LEGAL SERVICES

NOTARY LOGBOOK

This Logbook Belongs To:

_____

_____

❖ NOTARY LOGBOOK ❖   / 1

Printed Name :

Email Address :

Phone No. :

Address :

Signer's Signature :

Thumb Print :

Document Type :	Date Notarized :	Document Date :	Fee Charged :

ID Number :

Issued By :

Date Issued :	Expiration Date :

Identification :
- ☐ ID Card   ☐ Witness
- ☐ Known Personally
- ☐ Driver's License   ☐ Passport
- ☐ Others

Service Performed :
- ☐ Jurat   ☐ Oath
- ☐ Acknowledgement
- ☐ Others

Witness Name :	Address :
Email Address :	Phone No. :
Witness Signature :	NOTE :

❖ NOTARY LOGBOOK ❖   / 2

Printed Name :

Email Address :

Phone No. :

Address :

Signer's Signature :

Thumb Print :

Document Type :	Date Notarized :	Document Date :	Fee Charged :

ID Number :

Issued By :

Date Issued :	Expiration Date :

Identification :
- ☐ ID Card   ☐ Witness
- ☐ Known Personally
- ☐ Driver's License   ☐ Passport
- ☐ Others

Service Performed :
- ☐ Jurat   ☐ Oath
- ☐ Acknowledgement
- ☐ Others

Witness Name :	Address :
Email Address :	Phone No. :
Witness Signature :	NOTE :

� NOTARY LOGBOOK ⟩ 3

Printed Name :	Signer's Signature :	Thumb Print :
Email Address :		
Phone No. :		
Address :		

Document Type :	Date Notarized :	Document Date :	Fee Charged :

ID Number :	Identification :	Service Performed :
	☐ ID Card ☐ Witness	☐ Jurat ☐ Oath
	☐ Known Personally	☐ Acknowledgement
Issued By :	☐ Driver's License ☐ Passport	
	☐ Others	☐ Others
Date Issued : Expiration Date :		

Witness Name :	Address :
Email Address :	Phone No. :
Witness Signature :	NOTE :

⟩ NOTARY LOGBOOK ⟩ 4

Printed Name :	Signer's Signature :	Thumb Print :
Email Address :		
Phone No. :		
Address :		

Document Type :	Date Notarized :	Document Date :	Fee Charged :

ID Number :	Identification :	Service Performed :
	☐ ID Card ☐ Witness	☐ Jurat ☐ Oath
	☐ Known Personally	☐ Acknowledgement
Issued By :	☐ Driver's License ☐ Passport	
	☐ Others	☐ Others
Date Issued : Expiration Date :		

Witness Name :	Address :
Email Address :	Phone No. :
Witness Signature :	NOTE :

← NOTARY LOGBOOK ← / 5

Printed Name :	Signer's Signature :	Thumb Print :
Email Address :		
Phone No. :		
Address :		

Document Type :	Date Notarized :	Document Date :	Fee Charged :

ID Number :	Identification :	Service Performed :
	☐ ID Card ☐ Witness	☐ Jurat ☐ Oath
Issued By :	☐ Known Personally	☐ Acknowledgement
	☐ Driver's License ☐ Passport	
Date Issued : Expiration Date :	☐ Others	☐ Others

Witness Name :	Address :
Email Address :	Phone No. :
Witness Signature :	NOTE :

← NOTARY LOGBOOK ← / 6

Printed Name :	Signer's Signature :	Thumb Print :
Email Address :		
Phone No. :		
Address :		

Document Type :	Date Notarized :	Document Date :	Fee Charged :

ID Number :	Identification :	Service Performed :
	☐ ID Card ☐ Witness	☐ Jurat ☐ Oath
Issued By :	☐ Known Personally	☐ Acknowledgement
	☐ Driver's License ☐ Passport	
Date Issued : Expiration Date :	☐ Others	☐ Others

Witness Name :	Address :
Email Address :	Phone No. :
Witness Signature :	NOTE :

✦ NOTARY LOGBOOK ✦ / 7

Printed Name :

Email Address :

Phone No. :

Address :

Signer's Signature :

Thumb Print :

| Document Type : | Date Notarized : | Document Date : | Fee Charged : |

ID Number :

Issued By :

Date Issued : Expiration Date :

Identification :
- ☐ ID Card
- ☐ Known Personally
- ☐ Driver's License
- ☐ Witness
- ☐ Passport
- ☐ Others

Service Performed :
- ☐ Jurat
- ☐ Acknowledgement
- ☐ Oath
- ☐ Others

Witness Name :

Address :

Email Address :

Phone No. :

Witness Signature :

NOTE :

✦ NOTARY LOGBOOK ✦ / 8

Printed Name :

Email Address :

Phone No. :

Address :

Signer's Signature :

Thumb Print :

| Document Type : | Date Notarized : | Document Date : | Fee Charged : |

ID Number :

Issued By :

Date Issued : Expiration Date :

Identification :
- ☐ ID Card
- ☐ Known Personally
- ☐ Driver's License
- ☐ Witness
- ☐ Passport
- ☐ Others

Service Performed :
- ☐ Jurat
- ☐ Acknowledgement
- ☐ Oath
- ☐ Others

Witness Name :

Address :

Email Address :

Phone No. :

Witness Signature :

NOTE :

⤜ NOTARY LOGBOOK ⤛ / 9

Printed Name :	Signer's Signature :	Thumb Print :
Email Address :		
Phone No. :		
Address :		

Document Type :	Date Notarized :	Document Date :	Fee Charged :

ID Number :	Identification :	Service Performed :
	☐ ID Card ☐ Witness	☐ Jurat ☐ Oath
	☐ Known Personally	☐ Acknowledgement
Issued By :	☐ Driver's License ☐ Passport	
Date Issued : Expiration Date :	☐ Others	☐ Others

Witness Name :	Address :
Email Address :	Phone No. :
Witness Signature :	NOTE :

⤜ NOTARY LOGBOOK ⤛ / 10

Printed Name :	Signer's Signature :	Thumb Print :
Email Address :		
Phone No. :		
Address :		

Document Type :	Date Notarized :	Document Date :	Fee Charged :

ID Number :	Identification :	Service Performed :
	☐ ID Card ☐ Witness	☐ Jurat ☐ Oath
	☐ Known Personally	☐ Acknowledgement
Issued By :	☐ Driver's License ☐ Passport	
Date Issued : Expiration Date :	☐ Others	☐ Others

Witness Name :	Address :
Email Address :	Phone No. :
Witness Signature :	NOTE :

NOTARY LOGBOOK 11

Printed Name :

Email Address :

Phone No. :

Address :

Signer's Signature :

Thumb Print :

Document Type :	Date Notarized :	Document Date :	Fee Charged :

ID Number :

Issued By :

Date Issued :

Expiration Date :

Identification :

☐ ID Card ☐ Witness
☐ Known Personally
☐ Driver's License ☐ Passport
☐ Others

Service Performed :

☐ Jurat ☐ Oath
☐ Acknowledgement
☐ Others

Witness Name :

Address :

Email Address :

Phone No. :

Witness Signature :

NOTE :

NOTARY LOGBOOK 12

Printed Name :

Email Address :

Phone No. :

Address :

Signer's Signature :

Thumb Print :

Document Type :	Date Notarized :	Document Date :	Fee Charged :

ID Number :

Issued By :

Date Issued :

Expiration Date :

Identification :

☐ ID Card ☐ Witness
☐ Known Personally
☐ Driver's License ☐ Passport
☐ Others

Service Performed :

☐ Jurat ☐ Oath
☐ Acknowledgement
☐ Others

Witness Name :

Address :

Email Address :

Phone No. :

Witness Signature :

NOTE :

↔ NOTARY LOGBOOK ↔ / 13

Printed Name :

Email Address :

Phone No. :

Address :

Signer's Signature :

Thumb Print :

Document Type :	Date Notarized :	Document Date :	Fee Charged :

ID Number :

Issued By :

Date Issued :	Expiration Date :

Identification :
- ☐ ID Card   ☐ Witness
- ☐ Known Personally
- ☐ Driver's License ☐ Passport
- ☐ Others

Service Performed :
- ☐ Jurat   ☐ Oath
- ☐ Acknowledgement
- ☐ Others

Witness Name :	Address :
Email Address :	Phone No. :
Witness Signature :	NOTE :

↔ NOTARY LOGBOOK ↔ / 14

Printed Name :

Email Address :

Phone No. :

Address :

Signer's Signature :

Thumb Print :

Document Type :	Date Notarized :	Document Date :	Fee Charged :

ID Number :

Issued By :

Date Issued :	Expiration Date :

Identification :
- ☐ ID Card   ☐ Witness
- ☐ Known Personally
- ☐ Driver's License ☐ Passport
- ☐ Others

Service Performed :
- ☐ Jurat   ☐ Oath
- ☐ Acknowledgement
- ☐ Others

Witness Name :	Address :
Email Address :	Phone No. :
Witness Signature :	NOTE :

❖ NOTARY LOGBOOK ❖ / 15

Printed Name :

Email Address :

Phone No. :

Address :

Signer's Signature :

Thumb Print :

Document Type :	Date Notarized :	Document Date :	Fee Charged :

ID Number :

Issued By :

Date Issued :	Expiration Date :

Identification :
- [ ] ID Card
- [ ] Known Personally
- [ ] Driver's License
- [ ] Witness
- [ ] Passport
- [ ] Others

Service Performed :
- [ ] Jurat
- [ ] Oath
- [ ] Acknowledgement
- [ ] Others

Witness Name :

Email Address :

Witness Signature :

Address :

Phone No. :

NOTE :

❖ NOTARY LOGBOOK ❖ / 16

Printed Name :

Email Address :

Phone No. :

Address :

Signer's Signature :

Thumb Print :

Document Type :	Date Notarized :	Document Date :	Fee Charged :

ID Number :

Issued By :

Date Issued :	Expiration Date :

Identification :
- [ ] ID Card
- [ ] Known Personally
- [ ] Driver's License
- [ ] Witness
- [ ] Passport
- [ ] Others

Service Performed :
- [ ] Jurat
- [ ] Oath
- [ ] Acknowledgement
- [ ] Others

Witness Name :

Email Address :

Witness Signature :

Address :

Phone No. :

NOTE :

⇥ NOTARY LOGBOOK ⇤ 17

Printed Name :

Email Address :

Phone No. :

Address :

Signer's Signature :

Thumb Print :

Document Type :	Date Notarized :	Document Date :	Fee Charged :

ID Number :

Issued By :

Date Issued :	Expiration Date :

Identification :
- ☐ ID Card
- ☐ Witness
- ☐ Known Personally
- ☐ Driver's License
- ☐ Passport
- ☐ Others

Service Performed :
- ☐ Jurat
- ☐ Oath
- ☐ Acknowledgement
- ☐ Others

Witness Name :

Address :

Email Address :

Phone No. :

Witness Signature :

NOTE :

⇥ NOTARY LOGBOOK ⇤ 18

Printed Name :

Email Address :

Phone No. :

Address :

Signer's Signature :

Thumb Print :

Document Type :	Date Notarized :	Document Date :	Fee Charged :

ID Number :

Issued By :

Date Issued :	Expiration Date :

Identification :
- ☐ ID Card
- ☐ Witness
- ☐ Known Personally
- ☐ Driver's License
- ☐ Passport
- ☐ Others

Service Performed :
- ☐ Jurat
- ☐ Oath
- ☐ Acknowledgement
- ☐ Others

Witness Name :

Address :

Email Address :

Phone No. :

Witness Signature :

NOTE :

⤨ NOTARY LOGBOOK ⤨ / 19

Printed Name :

Email Address :

Phone No. :

Address :

Signer's Signature :

Thumb Print :

Document Type :	Date Notarized :	Document Date :	Fee Charged :

ID Number :	Identification :	Service Performed :

Identification :
- ☐ ID Card
- ☐ Known Personally
- ☐ Driver's License
- ☐ Witness
- ☐ Passport
- ☐ Others

Service Performed :
- ☐ Jurat
- ☐ Oath
- ☐ Acknowledgement
- ☐ Others

Issued By :

Date Issued :	Expiration Date :

Witness Name :

Email Address :

Witness Signature :

Address :

Phone No. :

NOTE :

⤨ NOTARY LOGBOOK ⤨ / 20

Printed Name :

Email Address :

Phone No. :

Address :

Signer's Signature :

Thumb Print :

Document Type :	Date Notarized :	Document Date :	Fee Charged :

ID Number :	Identification :	Service Performed :

Identification :
- ☐ ID Card
- ☐ Known Personally
- ☐ Driver's License
- ☐ Witness
- ☐ Passport
- ☐ Others

Service Performed :
- ☐ Jurat
- ☐ Oath
- ☐ Acknowledgement
- ☐ Others

Issued By :

Date Issued :	Expiration Date :

Witness Name :

Email Address :

Witness Signature :

Address :

Phone No. :

NOTE :

⤜ NOTARY LOGBOOK ⤛ / 21

Printed Name :

Signer's Signature :

Thumb Print :

Email Address :

Phone No. :

Address :

Document Type :	Date Notarized :	Document Date :	Fee Charged :

ID Number :

Issued By :

Date Issued :	Expiration Date :

Identification :
- ☐ ID Card
- ☐ Witness
- ☐ Known Personally
- ☐ Driver's License
- ☐ Passport
- ☐ Others

Service Performed :
- ☐ Jurat
- ☐ Oath
- ☐ Acknowledgement
- ☐ Others

Witness Name :

Address :

Email Address :

Phone No. :

Witness Signature :

NOTE :

⤜ NOTARY LOGBOOK ⤛ / 22

Printed Name :

Signer's Signature :

Thumb Print :

Email Address :

Phone No. :

Address :

Document Type :	Date Notarized :	Document Date :	Fee Charged :

ID Number :

Issued By :

Date Issued :	Expiration Date :

Identification :
- ☐ ID Card
- ☐ Witness
- ☐ Known Personally
- ☐ Driver's License
- ☐ Passport
- ☐ Others

Service Performed :
- ☐ Jurat
- ☐ Oath
- ☐ Acknowledgement
- ☐ Others

Witness Name :

Address :

Email Address :

Phone No. :

Witness Signature :

NOTE :

NOTARY LOGBOOK

Printed Name :

Signer's Signature :

Thumb Print :

Email Address :

Phone No. :

Address :

Document Type :	Date Notarized :	Document Date :	Fee Charged :

ID Number :

Identification :
- ☐ ID Card ☐ Witness
- ☐ Known Personally
- ☐ Driver's License ☐ Passport
- ☐ Others

Service Performed :
- ☐ Jurat ☐ Oath
- ☐ Acknowledgement
- ☐ Others

Issued By :

Date Issued :	Expiration Date :

Witness Name :	Address :
Email Address :	Phone No. :
Witness Signature :	NOTE :

NOTARY LOGBOOK

Printed Name :

Signer's Signature :

Thumb Print :

Email Address :

Phone No. :

Address :

Document Type :	Date Notarized :	Document Date :	Fee Charged :

ID Number :

Identification :
- ☐ ID Card ☐ Witness
- ☐ Known Personally
- ☐ Driver's License ☐ Passport
- ☐ Others

Service Performed :
- ☐ Jurat ☐ Oath
- ☐ Acknowledgement
- ☐ Others

Issued By :

Date Issued :	Expiration Date :

Witness Name :	Address :
Email Address :	Phone No. :
Witness Signature :	NOTE :

✦ NOTARY LOGBOOK ✦ / 25

Printed Name :

Email Address :

Phone No. :

Address :

Signer's Signature :

Thumb Print :

Document Type :	Date Notarized :	Document Date :	Fee Charged :

ID Number :

Issued By :

Date Issued :	Expiration Date :

Identification :
- ☐ ID Card   ☐ Witness
- ☐ Known Personally
- ☐ Driver's License ☐ Passport
- ☐ Others

Service Performed :
- ☐ Jurat   ☐ Oath
- ☐ Acknowledgement
- ☐ Others

Witness Name :	Address :
Email Address :	Phone No. :
Witness Signature :	NOTE :

✦ NOTARY LOGBOOK ✦ / 26

Printed Name :

Email Address :

Phone No. :

Address :

Signer's Signature :

Thumb Print :

Document Type :	Date Notarized :	Document Date :	Fee Charged :

ID Number :

Issued By :

Date Issued :	Expiration Date :

Identification :
- ☐ ID Card   ☐ Witness
- ☐ Known Personally
- ☐ Driver's License ☐ Passport
- ☐ Others

Service Performed :
- ☐ Jurat   ☐ Oath
- ☐ Acknowledgement
- ☐ Others

Witness Name :	Address :
Email Address :	Phone No. :
Witness Signature :	NOTE :

NOTARY LOGBOOK / 27

Printed Name :

Email Address :

Phone No. :

Address :

Signer's Signature :

Thumb Print :

Document Type :	Date Notarized :	Document Date :	Fee Charged :

ID Number :

Issued By :

Date Issued :	Expiration Date :

Identification :
- ☐ ID Card
- ☐ Known Personally
- ☐ Driver's License
- ☐ Witness
- ☐ Passport
- ☐ Others

Service Performed :
- ☐ Jurat
- ☐ Oath
- ☐ Acknowledgement
- ☐ Others

Witness Name :

Email Address :

Witness Signature :

Address :

Phone No. :

NOTE :

NOTARY LOGBOOK / 28

Printed Name :

Email Address :

Phone No. :

Address :

Signer's Signature :

Thumb Print :

Document Type :	Date Notarized :	Document Date :	Fee Charged :

ID Number :

Issued By :

Date Issued :	Expiration Date :

Identification :
- ☐ ID Card
- ☐ Known Personally
- ☐ Driver's License
- ☐ Witness
- ☐ Passport
- ☐ Others

Service Performed :
- ☐ Jurat
- ☐ Oath
- ☐ Acknowledgement
- ☐ Others

Witness Name :

Email Address :

Witness Signature :

Address :

Phone No. :

NOTE :

Printed Name :

Email Address :

Phone No. :

Address :

Signer's Signature :

Thumb Print :

Document Type :	Date Notarized :	Document Date :	Fee Charged :

ID Number :

Issued By :

Date Issued :	Expiration Date :

Identification :
- ☐ ID Card   ☐ Witness
- ☐ Known Personally
- ☐ Driver's License   ☐ Passport
- ☐ Others

Service Performed :
- ☐ Jurat   ☐ Oath
- ☐ Acknowledgement
- ☐ Others

Witness Name :

Email Address :

Witness Signature :

Address :

Phone No. :

NOTE :

Printed Name :

Email Address :

Phone No. :

Address :

Signer's Signature :

Thumb Print :

Document Type :	Date Notarized :	Document Date :	Fee Charged :

ID Number :

Issued By :

Date Issued :	Expiration Date :

Identification :
- ☐ ID Card   ☐ Witness
- ☐ Known Personally
- ☐ Driver's License   ☐ Passport
- ☐ Others

Service Performed :
- ☐ Jurat   ☐ Oath
- ☐ Acknowledgement
- ☐ Others

Witness Name :

Email Address :

Witness Signature :

Address :

Phone No. :

NOTE :

NOTARY LOGBOOK

Printed Name :

Email Address :

Phone No. :

Address :

Signer's Signature :

Thumb Print :

Document Type :	Date Notarized :	Document Date :	Fee Charged :

ID Number :

Issued By :

Date Issued :	Expiration Date :

Identification :
- ☐ ID Card
- ☐ Witness
- ☐ Known Personally
- ☐ Driver's License
- ☐ Passport
- ☐ Others

Service Performed :
- ☐ Jurat
- ☐ Oath
- ☐ Acknowledgement
- ☐ Others

Witness Name :

Email Address :

Witness Signature :

Address :

Phone No. :

NOTE :

NOTARY LOGBOOK

Printed Name :

Email Address :

Phone No. :

Address :

Signer's Signature :

Thumb Print :

Document Type :	Date Notarized :	Document Date :	Fee Charged :

ID Number :

Issued By :

Date Issued :	Expiration Date :

Identification :
- ☐ ID Card
- ☐ Witness
- ☐ Known Personally
- ☐ Driver's License
- ☐ Passport
- ☐ Others

Service Performed :
- ☐ Jurat
- ☐ Oath
- ☐ Acknowledgement
- ☐ Others

Witness Name :

Email Address :

Witness Signature :

Address :

Phone No. :

NOTE :

⤞ NOTARY LOGBOOK ⤝   / 33

Printed Name :

Email Address :

Phone No. :

Address :

Signer's Signature :

Thumb Print :

Document Type :	Date Notarized :	Document Date :	Fee Charged :

ID Number :

Issued By :

Date Issued :	Expiration Date :

Identification :
- ☐ ID Card   ☐ Witness
- ☐ Known Personally
- ☐ Driver's License ☐ Passport
- ☐ Others

Service Performed :
- ☐ Jurat   ☐ Oath
- ☐ Acknowledgement
- ☐ Others

Witness Name :

Email Address :

Witness Signature :

Address :

Phone No. :

NOTE :

⤞ NOTARY LOGBOOK ⤝   / 34

Printed Name :

Email Address :

Phone No. :

Address :

Signer's Signature :

Thumb Print :

Document Type :	Date Notarized :	Document Date :	Fee Charged :

ID Number :

Issued By :

Date Issued :	Expiration Date :

Identification :
- ☐ ID Card   ☐ Witness
- ☐ Known Personally
- ☐ Driver's License ☐ Passport
- ☐ Others

Service Performed :
- ☐ Jurat   ☐ Oath
- ☐ Acknowledgement
- ☐ Others

Witness Name :

Email Address :

Witness Signature :

Address :

Phone No. :

NOTE :

NOTARY LOGBOOK

Printed Name :

Email Address :

Phone No. :

Address :

Signer's Signature :

Thumb Print :

Document Type :	Date Notarized :	Document Date :	Fee Charged :

ID Number :

Issued By :

Date Issued :	Expiration Date :

Identification :
- ☐ ID Card   ☐ Witness
- ☐ Known Personally
- ☐ Driver's License   ☐ Passport
- ☐ Others

Service Performed :
- ☐ Jurat   ☐ Oath
- ☐ Acknowledgement
- ☐ Others

Witness Name :

Email Address :

Witness Signature :

Address :

Phone No. :

NOTE :

NOTARY LOGBOOK

Printed Name :

Email Address :

Phone No. :

Address :

Signer's Signature :

Thumb Print :

Document Type :	Date Notarized :	Document Date :	Fee Charged :

ID Number :

Issued By :

Date Issued :	Expiration Date :

Identification :
- ☐ ID Card   ☐ Witness
- ☐ Known Personally
- ☐ Driver's License   ☐ Passport
- ☐ Others

Service Performed :
- ☐ Jurat   ☐ Oath
- ☐ Acknowledgement
- ☐ Others

Witness Name :

Email Address :

Witness Signature :

Address :

Phone No. :

NOTE :

✦ NOTARY LOGBOOK ✦ / 37

Printed Name :

Email Address :

Phone No. :

Address :

Signer's Signature :

Thumb Print :

Document Type :	Date Notarized :	Document Date :	Fee Charged :

ID Number :

Issued By :

Date Issued :	Expiration Date :

Identification :
- ☐ ID Card
- ☐ Witness
- ☐ Known Personally
- ☐ Driver's License
- ☐ Passport
- ☐ Others

Service Performed :
- ☐ Jurat
- ☐ Oath
- ☐ Acknowledgement
- ☐ Others

Witness Name :

Email Address :

Witness Signature :

Address :

Phone No. :

NOTE :

✦ NOTARY LOGBOOK ✦ / 38

Printed Name :

Email Address :

Phone No. :

Address :

Signer's Signature :

Thumb Print :

Document Type :	Date Notarized :	Document Date :	Fee Charged :

ID Number :

Issued By :

Date Issued :	Expiration Date :

Identification :
- ☐ ID Card
- ☐ Witness
- ☐ Known Personally
- ☐ Driver's License
- ☐ Passport
- ☐ Others

Service Performed :
- ☐ Jurat
- ☐ Oath
- ☐ Acknowledgement
- ☐ Others

Witness Name :

Email Address :

Witness Signature :

Address :

Phone No. :

NOTE :

✦ NOTARY LOGBOOK ✦ 39

Printed Name :

Signer's Signature :

Thumb Print :

Email Address :

Phone No. :

Address :

Document Type :	Date Notarized :	Document Date :	Fee Charged :

ID Number :

Identification :
- ☐ ID Card
- ☐ Known Personally
- ☐ Driver's License
- ☐ Witness
- ☐ Passport
- ☐ Others

Service Performed :
- ☐ Jurat
- ☐ Oath
- ☐ Acknowledgement
- ☐ Others

Issued By :

Date Issued :	Expiration Date :

Witness Name :

Address :

Email Address :

Phone No. :

Witness Signature :

NOTE :

✦ NOTARY LOGBOOK ✦ 40

Printed Name :

Signer's Signature :

Thumb Print :

Email Address :

Phone No. :

Address :

Document Type :	Date Notarized :	Document Date :	Fee Charged :

ID Number :

Identification :
- ☐ ID Card
- ☐ Known Personally
- ☐ Driver's License
- ☐ Witness
- ☐ Passport
- ☐ Others

Service Performed :
- ☐ Jurat
- ☐ Oath
- ☐ Acknowledgement
- ☐ Others

Issued By :

Date Issued :	Expiration Date :

Witness Name :

Address :

Email Address :

Phone No. :

Witness Signature :

NOTE :

✦ NOTARY LOGBOOK ✦ / 41

Printed Name :

Email Address :

Phone No. :

Address :

Signer's Signature :

Thumb Print :

Document Type :	Date Notarized :	Document Date :	Fee Charged :

ID Number :

Issued By :

Date Issued :　Expiration Date :

Identification :
- ☐ ID Card　☐ Witness
- ☐ Known Personally
- ☐ Driver's License　☐ Passport
- ☐ Others

Service Performed :
- ☐ Jurat　☐ Oath
- ☐ Acknowledgement
- ☐ Others

Witness Name :

Email Address :

Witness Signature :

Address :

Phone No. :

NOTE :

✦ NOTARY LOGBOOK ✦ / 42

Printed Name :

Email Address :

Phone No. :

Address :

Signer's Signature :

Thumb Print :

Document Type :	Date Notarized :	Document Date :	Fee Charged :

ID Number :

Issued By :

Date Issued :　Expiration Date :

Identification :
- ☐ ID Card　☐ Witness
- ☐ Known Personally
- ☐ Driver's License　☐ Passport
- ☐ Others

Service Performed :
- ☐ Jurat　☐ Oath
- ☐ Acknowledgement
- ☐ Others

Witness Name :

Email Address :

Witness Signature :

Address :

Phone No. :

NOTE :

NOTARY LOGBOOK 43

Printed Name :

Email Address :

Phone No. :

Address :

Signer's Signature :

Thumb Print :

Document Type :	Date Notarized :	Document Date :	Fee Charged :

ID Number :

Issued By :

Date Issued :	Expiration Date :

Identification :
- ☐ ID Card
- ☐ Known Personally
- ☐ Driver's License
- ☐ Witness
- ☐ Passport
- ☐ Others

Service Performed :
- ☐ Jurat
- ☐ Oath
- ☐ Acknowledgement
- ☐ Others

Witness Name :

Address :

Email Address :

Phone No. :

Witness Signature :

NOTE :

NOTARY LOGBOOK 44

Printed Name :

Email Address :

Phone No. :

Address :

Signer's Signature :

Thumb Print :

Document Type :	Date Notarized :	Document Date :	Fee Charged :

ID Number :

Issued By :

Date Issued :	Expiration Date :

Identification :
- ☐ ID Card
- ☐ Known Personally
- ☐ Driver's License
- ☐ Witness
- ☐ Passport
- ☐ Others

Service Performed :
- ☐ Jurat
- ☐ Oath
- ☐ Acknowledgement
- ☐ Others

Witness Name :

Address :

Email Address :

Phone No. :

Witness Signature :

NOTE :

✦ NOTARY LOGBOOK ✦ / 45

Printed Name :

Email Address :

Phone No. :

Address :

Signer's Signature :

Thumb Print :

Document Type :	Date Notarized :	Document Date :	Fee Charged :

ID Number :

Issued By :

Date Issued :	Expiration Date :

Identification :
- ☐ ID Card
- ☐ Known Personally
- ☐ Driver's License
- ☐ Witness
- ☐ Passport
- ☐ Others

Service Performed :
- ☐ Jurat
- ☐ Oath
- ☐ Acknowledgement
- ☐ Others

Witness Name :

Address :

Email Address :

Phone No. :

Witness Signature :

NOTE :

✦ NOTARY LOGBOOK ✦ / 46

Printed Name :

Email Address :

Phone No. :

Address :

Signer's Signature :

Thumb Print :

Document Type :	Date Notarized :	Document Date :	Fee Charged :

ID Number :

Issued By :

Date Issued :	Expiration Date :

Identification :
- ☐ ID Card
- ☐ Known Personally
- ☐ Driver's License
- ☐ Witness
- ☐ Passport
- ☐ Others

Service Performed :
- ☐ Jurat
- ☐ Oath
- ☐ Acknowledgement
- ☐ Others

Witness Name :

Address :

Email Address :

Phone No. :

Witness Signature :

NOTE :

⤜ NOTARY LOGBOOK ⤛ / 47

Printed Name :

Email Address :

Phone No. :

Address :

Signer's Signature :

Thumb Print :

Document Type :	Date Notarized :	Document Date :	Fee Charged :

ID Number :

Issued By :

Date Issued :	Expiration Date :

Identification :
- ☐ ID Card   ☐ Witness
- ☐ Known Personally
- ☐ Driver's License   ☐ Passport
- ☐ Others

Service Performed :
- ☐ Jurat   ☐ Oath
- ☐ Acknowledgement
- ☐ Others

Witness Name :

Email Address :

Witness Signature :

Address :

Phone No. :

NOTE :

⤜ NOTARY LOGBOOK ⤛ / 48

Printed Name :

Email Address :

Phone No. :

Address :

Signer's Signature :

Thumb Print :

Document Type :	Date Notarized :	Document Date :	Fee Charged :

ID Number :

Issued By :

Date Issued :	Expiration Date :

Identification :
- ☐ ID Card   ☐ Witness
- ☐ Known Personally
- ☐ Driver's License   ☐ Passport
- ☐ Others

Service Performed :
- ☐ Jurat   ☐ Oath
- ☐ Acknowledgement
- ☐ Others

Witness Name :

Email Address :

Witness Signature :

Address :

Phone No. :

NOTE :

Printed Name :

Signer's Signature :

Thumb Print :

Email Address :

Phone No. :

Address :

Document Type :	Date Notarized :	Document Date :	Fee Charged :

ID Number :

Issued By :

Date Issued :	Expiration Date :

Identification :
- ☐ ID Card   ☐ Witness
- ☐ Known Personally
- ☐ Driver's License   ☐ Passport
- ☐ Others

Service Performed :
- ☐ Jurat   ☐ Oath
- ☐ Acknowledgement
- ☐ Others

Witness Name :

Address :

Email Address :

Phone No. :

Witness Signature :

NOTE :

Printed Name :

Signer's Signature :

Thumb Print :

Email Address :

Phone No. :

Address :

Document Type :	Date Notarized :	Document Date :	Fee Charged :

ID Number :

Issued By :

Date Issued :	Expiration Date :

Identification :
- ☐ ID Card   ☐ Witness
- ☐ Known Personally
- ☐ Driver's License   ☐ Passport
- ☐ Others

Service Performed :
- ☐ Jurat   ☐ Oath
- ☐ Acknowledgement
- ☐ Others

Witness Name :

Address :

Email Address :

Phone No. :

Witness Signature :

NOTE :

☙ NOTARY LOGBOOK ☙ / 51

Printed Name :

Email Address :

Phone No. :

Address :

Signer's Signature :

Thumb Print :

Document Type :	Date Notarized :	Document Date :	Fee Charged :

ID Number :

Issued By :

Date Issued :	Expiration Date :

Identification :
- ☐ ID Card   ☐ Witness
- ☐ Known Personally
- ☐ Driver's License ☐ Passport
- ☐ Others

Service Performed :
- ☐ Jurat   ☐ Oath
- ☐ Acknowledgement
- ☐ Others

Witness Name :

Email Address :

Witness Signature :

Address :

Phone No. :

NOTE :

☙ NOTARY LOGBOOK ☙ / 52

Printed Name :

Email Address :

Phone No. :

Address :

Signer's Signature :

Thumb Print :

Document Type :	Date Notarized :	Document Date :	Fee Charged :

ID Number :

Issued By :

Date Issued :	Expiration Date :

Identification :
- ☐ ID Card   ☐ Witness
- ☐ Known Personally
- ☐ Driver's License ☐ Passport
- ☐ Others

Service Performed :
- ☐ Jurat   ☐ Oath
- ☐ Acknowledgement
- ☐ Others

Witness Name :

Email Address :

Witness Signature :

Address :

Phone No. :

NOTE :

✦ NOTARY LOGBOOK ✦ / 53

Printed Name :

Email Address :

Phone No. :

Address :

Signer's Signature :

Thumb Print :

Document Type :	Date Notarized :	Document Date :	Fee Charged :

ID Number :

Issued By :

Date Issued :	Expiration Date :

Identification :
- ☐ ID Card   ☐ Witness
- ☐ Known Personally
- ☐ Driver's License   ☐ Passport
- ☐ Others

Service Performed :
- ☐ Jurat   ☐ Oath
- ☐ Acknowledgement
- ☐ Others

Witness Name :

Address :

Email Address :

Phone No. :

Witness Signature :

NOTE :

✦ NOTARY LOGBOOK ✦ / 54

Printed Name :

Email Address :

Phone No. :

Address :

Signer's Signature :

Thumb Print :

Document Type :	Date Notarized :	Document Date :	Fee Charged :

ID Number :

Issued By :

Date Issued :	Expiration Date :

Identification :
- ☐ ID Card   ☐ Witness
- ☐ Known Personally
- ☐ Driver's License   ☐ Passport
- ☐ Others

Service Performed :
- ☐ Jurat   ☐ Oath
- ☐ Acknowledgement
- ☐ Others

Witness Name :

Address :

Email Address :

Phone No. :

Witness Signature :

NOTE :

→ NOTARY LOGBOOK ← / 55

Printed Name :

Email Address :

Phone No. :

Address :

Signer's Signature :

Thumb Print :

Document Type :	Date Notarized :	Document Date :	Fee Charged :

ID Number :

Issued By :

Date Issued :	Expiration Date :

Identification :
- ☐ ID Card   ☐ Witness
- ☐ Known Personally
- ☐ Driver's License ☐ Passport
- ☐ Others

Service Performed :
- ☐ Jurat   ☐ Oath
- ☐ Acknowledgement
- ☐ Others

Witness Name :

Email Address :

Witness Signature :

Address :

Phone No. :

NOTE :

→ NOTARY LOGBOOK ← / 56

Printed Name :

Email Address :

Phone No. :

Address :

Signer's Signature :

Thumb Print :

Document Type :	Date Notarized :	Document Date :	Fee Charged :

ID Number :

Issued By :

Date Issued :	Expiration Date :

Identification :
- ☐ ID Card   ☐ Witness
- ☐ Known Personally
- ☐ Driver's License ☐ Passport
- ☐ Others

Service Performed :
- ☐ Jurat   ☐ Oath
- ☐ Acknowledgement
- ☐ Others

Witness Name :

Email Address :

Witness Signature :

Address :

Phone No. :

NOTE :

NOTARY LOGBOOK 57

Printed Name :

Email Address :

Phone No. :

Address :

Signer's Signature :

Thumb Print :

Document Type :	Date Notarized :	Document Date :	Fee Charged :

ID Number :

Issued By :

Date Issued :

Expiration Date :

Identification :
- ☐ ID Card
- ☐ Known Personally
- ☐ Driver's License
- ☐ Witness
- ☐ Passport
- ☐ Others

Service Performed :
- ☐ Jurat
- ☐ Oath
- ☐ Acknowledgement
- ☐ Others

Witness Name :

Email Address :

Witness Signature :

Address :

Phone No. :

NOTE :

NOTARY LOGBOOK 58

Printed Name :

Email Address :

Phone No. :

Address :

Signer's Signature :

Thumb Print :

Document Type :	Date Notarized :	Document Date :	Fee Charged :

ID Number :

Issued By :

Date Issued :

Expiration Date :

Identification :
- ☐ ID Card
- ☐ Known Personally
- ☐ Driver's License
- ☐ Witness
- ☐ Passport
- ☐ Others

Service Performed :
- ☐ Jurat
- ☐ Oath
- ☐ Acknowledgement
- ☐ Others

Witness Name :

Email Address :

Witness Signature :

Address :

Phone No. :

NOTE :

Printed Name :

Email Address :

Phone No. :

Address :

Signer's Signature :

Thumb Print :

Document Type :	Date Notarized :	Document Date :	Fee Charged :

ID Number :

Issued By :

Date Issued : | Expiration Date :

Identification :
- ☐ ID Card
- ☐ Witness
- ☐ Known Personally
- ☐ Driver's License
- ☐ Passport
- ☐ Others

Service Performed :
- ☐ Jurat
- ☐ Oath
- ☐ Acknowledgement
- ☐ Others

Witness Name :

Email Address :

Witness Signature :

Address :

Phone No. :

NOTE :

Printed Name :

Email Address :

Phone No. :

Address :

Signer's Signature :

Thumb Print :

Document Type :	Date Notarized :	Document Date :	Fee Charged :

ID Number :

Issued By :

Date Issued : | Expiration Date :

Identification :
- ☐ ID Card
- ☐ Witness
- ☐ Known Personally
- ☐ Driver's License
- ☐ Passport
- ☐ Others

Service Performed :
- ☐ Jurat
- ☐ Oath
- ☐ Acknowledgement
- ☐ Others

Witness Name :

Email Address :

Witness Signature :

Address :

Phone No. :

NOTE :

Printed Name :

Email Address :

Phone No. :

Address :

Signer's Signature :

Thumb Print :

Document Type :	Date Notarized :	Document Date :	Fee Charged :

ID Number :

Issued By :

Date Issued :	Expiration Date :

Identification :
- ☐ ID Card
- ☐ Witness
- ☐ Known Personally
- ☐ Driver's License
- ☐ Passport
- ☐ Others

Service Performed :
- ☐ Jurat
- ☐ Oath
- ☐ Acknowledgement
- ☐ Others

Witness Name :	Address :
Email Address :	Phone No. :
Witness Signature :	NOTE :

Printed Name :

Email Address :

Phone No. :

Address :

Signer's Signature :

Thumb Print :

Document Type :	Date Notarized :	Document Date :	Fee Charged :

ID Number :

Issued By :

Date Issued :	Expiration Date :

Identification :
- ☐ ID Card
- ☐ Witness
- ☐ Known Personally
- ☐ Driver's License
- ☐ Passport
- ☐ Others

Service Performed :
- ☐ Jurat
- ☐ Oath
- ☐ Acknowledgement
- ☐ Others

Witness Name :	Address :
Email Address :	Phone No. :
Witness Signature :	NOTE :

✦ NOTARY LOGBOOK ✦ / 63

Printed Name :

Email Address :

Phone No. :

Address :

Signer's Signature :

Thumb Print :

Document Type :	Date Notarized :	Document Date :	Fee Charged :

ID Number :

Issued By :

Date Issued :   Expiration Date :

Identification :
- ☐ ID Card   ☐ Witness
- ☐ Known Personally
- ☐ Driver's License   ☐ Passport
- ☐ Others

Service Performed :
- ☐ Jurat   ☐ Oath
- ☐ Acknowledgement
- ☐ Others

Witness Name :

Email Address :

Witness Signature :

Address :

Phone No. :

NOTE :

✦ NOTARY LOGBOOK ✦ / 64

Printed Name :

Email Address :

Phone No. :

Address :

Signer's Signature :

Thumb Print :

Document Type :	Date Notarized :	Document Date :	Fee Charged :

ID Number :

Issued By :

Date Issued :   Expiration Date :

Identification :
- ☐ ID Card   ☐ Witness
- ☐ Known Personally
- ☐ Driver's License   ☐ Passport
- ☐ Others

Service Performed :
- ☐ Jurat   ☐ Oath
- ☐ Acknowledgement
- ☐ Others

Witness Name :

Email Address :

Witness Signature :

Address :

Phone No. :

NOTE :

⤞ NOTARY LOGBOOK ⤝ / 65

Printed Name :

Email Address :

Phone No. :

Address :

Signer's Signature :

Thumb Print :

Document Type :	Date Notarized :	Document Date :	Fee Charged :

ID Number :

Issued By :

Date Issued :

Expiration Date :

Identification :
- ☐ ID Card
- ☐ Known Personally
- ☐ Driver's License
- ☐ Witness
- ☐ Passport
- ☐ Others

Service Performed :
- ☐ Jurat
- ☐ Oath
- ☐ Acknowledgement
- ☐ Others

Witness Name :

Address :

Email Address :

Phone No. :

Witness Signature :

NOTE :

⤞ NOTARY LOGBOOK ⤝ / 66

Printed Name :

Email Address :

Phone No. :

Address :

Signer's Signature :

Thumb Print :

Document Type :	Date Notarized :	Document Date :	Fee Charged :

ID Number :

Issued By :

Date Issued :

Expiration Date :

Identification :
- ☐ ID Card
- ☐ Known Personally
- ☐ Driver's License
- ☐ Witness
- ☐ Passport
- ☐ Others

Service Performed :
- ☐ Jurat
- ☐ Oath
- ☐ Acknowledgement
- ☐ Others

Witness Name :

Address :

Email Address :

Phone No. :

Witness Signature :

NOTE :

Printed Name :

Email Address :

Phone No. :

Address :

Signer's Signature :

Thumb Print :

Document Type :	Date Notarized :	Document Date :	Fee Charged :

ID Number :

Issued By :

Date Issued :   Expiration Date :

Identification :

☐ ID Card   ☐ Witness
☐ Known Personally
☐ Driver's License   ☐ Passport
☐ Others

Service Performed :

☐ Jurat   ☐ Oath
☐ Acknowledgement

☐ Others

Witness Name :   Address :

Email Address :   Phone No. :

Witness Signature :   NOTE :

Printed Name :

Email Address :

Phone No. :

Address :

Signer's Signature :

Thumb Print :

Document Type :	Date Notarized :	Document Date :	Fee Charged :

ID Number :

Issued By :

Date Issued :   Expiration Date :

Identification :

☐ ID Card   ☐ Witness
☐ Known Personally
☐ Driver's License   ☐ Passport
☐ Others

Service Performed :

☐ Jurat   ☐ Oath
☐ Acknowledgement

☐ Others

Witness Name :   Address :

Email Address :   Phone No. :

Witness Signature :   NOTE :

➤ NOTARY LOGBOOK ➤ / 69

Printed Name :

Email Address :

Phone No. :

Address :

Signer's Signature :

Thumb Print :

Document Type :	Date Notarized :	Document Date :	Fee Charged :

ID Number :

Issued By :

Date Issued :　Expiration Date :

Identification :
- ☐ ID Card　　☐ Witness
- ☐ Known Personally
- ☐ Driver's License　☐ Passport
- ☐ Others

Service Performed :
- ☐ Jurat　　☐ Oath
- ☐ Acknowledgement
- ☐ Others

Witness Name :

Email Address :

Witness Signature :

Address :

Phone No. :

NOTE :

➤ NOTARY LOGBOOK ➤ / 70

Printed Name :

Email Address :

Phone No. :

Address :

Signer's Signature :

Thumb Print :

Document Type :	Date Notarized :	Document Date :	Fee Charged :

ID Number :

Issued By :

Date Issued :　Expiration Date :

Identification :
- ☐ ID Card　　☐ Witness
- ☐ Known Personally
- ☐ Driver's License　☐ Passport
- ☐ Others

Service Performed :
- ☐ Jurat　　☐ Oath
- ☐ Acknowledgement
- ☐ Others

Witness Name :

Email Address :

Witness Signature :

Address :

Phone No. :

NOTE :

⇥ NOTARY LOGBOOK ⇤ / 71

Printed Name :

Email Address :

Phone No. :

Address :

Signer's Signature :

Thumb Print :

Document Type :	Date Notarized :	Document Date :	Fee Charged :

ID Number :

Issued By :

Date Issued :	Expiration Date :

Identification :
- ☐ ID Card   ☐ Witness
- ☐ Known Personally
- ☐ Driver's License   ☐ Passport
- ☐ Others

Service Performed :
- ☐ Jurat   ☐ Oath
- ☐ Acknowledgement
- ☐ Others

Witness Name :

Email Address :

Witness Signature :

Address :

Phone No. :

NOTE :

⇥ NOTARY LOGBOOK ⇤ / 72

Printed Name :

Email Address :

Phone No. :

Address :

Signer's Signature :

Thumb Print :

Document Type :	Date Notarized :	Document Date :	Fee Charged :

ID Number :

Issued By :

Date Issued :	Expiration Date :

Identification :
- ☐ ID Card   ☐ Witness
- ☐ Known Personally
- ☐ Driver's License   ☐ Passport
- ☐ Others

Service Performed :
- ☐ Jurat   ☐ Oath
- ☐ Acknowledgement
- ☐ Others

Witness Name :

Email Address :

Witness Signature :

Address :

Phone No. :

NOTE :

Printed Name :

Email Address :

Phone No. :

Address :

Signer's Signature :

Thumb Print :

Document Type :	Date Notarized :	Document Date :	Fee Charged :

ID Number :

Issued By :

Date Issued :	Expiration Date :

Identification :
- ☐ ID Card
- ☐ Known Personally
- ☐ Driver's License
- ☐ Witness
- ☐ Passport
- ☐ Others

Service Performed :
- ☐ Jurat
- ☐ Oath
- ☐ Acknowledgement
- ☐ Others

Witness Name :

Email Address :

Witness Signature :

Address :

Phone No. :

NOTE :

Printed Name :

Email Address :

Phone No. :

Address :

Signer's Signature :

Thumb Print :

Document Type :	Date Notarized :	Document Date :	Fee Charged :

ID Number :

Issued By :

Date Issued :	Expiration Date :

Identification :
- ☐ ID Card
- ☐ Known Personally
- ☐ Driver's License
- ☐ Witness
- ☐ Passport
- ☐ Others

Service Performed :
- ☐ Jurat
- ☐ Oath
- ☐ Acknowledgement
- ☐ Others

Witness Name :

Email Address :

Witness Signature :

Address :

Phone No. :

NOTE :

NOTARY LOGBOOK

Printed Name :

Signer's Signature :

Thumb Print :

Email Address :

Phone No. :

Address :

Document Type :	Date Notarized :	Document Date :	Fee Charged :

ID Number :

Issued By :

Date Issued :	Expiration Date :

Identification :
- ☐ ID Card ☐ Witness
- ☐ Known Personally
- ☐ Driver's License ☐ Passport
- ☐ Others

Service Performed :
- ☐ Jurat ☐ Oath
- ☐ Acknowledgement
- ☐ Others

Witness Name :	Address :
Email Address :	Phone No. :
Witness Signature :	NOTE :

NOTARY LOGBOOK

Printed Name :

Signer's Signature :

Thumb Print :

Email Address :

Phone No. :

Adrdess :

Document Type :	Date Notarized :	Document Date :	Fee Charged :

ID Number :

Issued By :

Date Issued :	Expiration Date :

Identification :
- ☐ ID Card ☐ Witness
- ☐ Known Personally
- ☐ Driver's License ☐ Passport
- ☐ Others

Service Performed :
- ☐ Jurat ☐ Oath
- ☐ Acknowledgement
- ☐ Others

Witness Name :	Address :
Email Address :	Phone No. :
Witness Signature :	NOTE :

Printed Name :	Signer's Signature :	Thumb Print :
Email Address :		
Phone No. :		
Address :		

Document Type :	Date Notarized :	Document Date :	Fee Charged :

ID Number :	Identification :	Service Performed :
Issued By :	☐ ID Card ☐ Witness ☐ Known Personally ☐ Driver's License ☐ Passport ☐ Others	☐ Jurat ☐ Oath ☐ Acknowledgement ☐ Others
Date Issued : Expiration Date :		

Witness Name :	Address :
Email Address :	Phone No. :
Witness Signature :	NOTE :

Printed Name :	Signer's Signature :	Thumb Print :
Email Address :		
Phone No. :		
Address :		

Document Type :	Date Notarized :	Document Date :	Fee Charged :

ID Number :	Identification :	Service Performed :
Issued By :	☐ ID Card ☐ Witness ☐ Known Personally ☐ Driver's License ☐ Passport ☐ Others	☐ Jurat ☐ Oath ☐ Acknowledgement ☐ Others
Date Issued : Expiration Date :		

Witness Name :	Address :
Email Address :	Phone No. :
Witness Signature :	NOTE :

Printed Name :

Email Address :

Phone No. :

Address :

Signer's Signature :

Thumb Print :

Document Type :	Date Notarized :	Document Date :	Fee Charged :

ID Number :

Issued By :

Date Issued :	Expiration Date :

Identification :
- ☐ ID Card   ☐ Witness
- ☐ Known Personally
- ☐ Driver's License   ☐ Passport
- ☐ Others

Service Performed :
- ☐ Jurat   ☐ Oath
- ☐ Acknowledgement
- ☐ Others

Witness Name :

Email Address :

Witness Signature :

Address :

Phone No. :

NOTE :

Printed Name :

Email Address :

Phone No. :

Address :

Signer's Signature :

Thumb Print :

Document Type :	Date Notarized :	Document Date :	Fee Charged :

ID Number :

Issued By :

Date Issued :	Expiration Date :

Identification :
- ☐ ID Card   ☐ Witness
- ☐ Known Personally
- ☐ Driver's License   ☐ Passport
- ☐ Others

Service Performed :
- ☐ Jurat   ☐ Oath
- ☐ Acknowledgement
- ☐ Others

Witness Name :

Email Address :

Witness Signature :

Address :

Phone No. :

NOTE :

⤜ NOTARY LOGBOOK ⤛ / 81

Printed Name :

Email Address :

Phone No. :

Address :

Signer's Signature :

Thumb Print :

Document Type :	Date Notarized :	Document Date :	Fee Charged :

ID Number :

Issued By :

Date Issued :　Expiration Date :

Identification :
- ☐ ID Card　☐ Witness
- ☐ Known Personally
- ☐ Driver's License　☐ Passport
- ☐ Others

Service Performed :
- ☐ Jurat　☐ Oath
- ☐ Acknowledgement
- ☐ Others

Witness Name :

Email Address :

Witness Signature :

Address :

Phone No. :

NOTE :

⤜ NOTARY LOGBOOK ⤛ / 82

Printed Name :

Email Address :

Phone No. :

Address :

Signer's Signature :

Thumb Print :

Document Type :	Date Notarized :	Document Date :	Fee Charged :

ID Number :

Issued By :

Date Issued :　Expiration Date :

Identification :
- ☐ ID Card　☐ Witness
- ☐ Known Personally
- ☐ Driver's License　☐ Passport
- ☐ Others

Service Performed :
- ☐ Jurat　☐ Oath
- ☐ Acknowledgement
- ☐ Others

Witness Name :

Email Address :

Witness Signature :

Address :

Phone No. :

NOTE :

⇥ NOTARY LOGBOOK ⇤ / 83

Printed Name :

Email Address :

Phone No. :

Address :

Signer's Signature :

Thumb Print :

Document Type :	Date Notarized :	Document Date :	Fee Charged :

ID Number :

Issued By :

Date Issued :　Expiration Date :

Identification :
- ☐ ID Card　☐ Witness
- ☐ Known Personally
- ☐ Driver's License　☐ Passport
- ☐ Others

Service Performed :
- ☐ Jurat　☐ Oath
- ☐ Acknowledgement
- ☐ Others

Witness Name :

Email Address :

Witness Signature :

Address :

Phone No. :

NOTE :

⇥ NOTARY LOGBOOK ⇤ / 84

Printed Name :

Email Address :

Phone No. :

Address :

Signer's Signature :

Thumb Print :

Document Type :	Date Notarized :	Document Date :	Fee Charged :

ID Number :

Issued By :

Date Issued :　Expiration Date :

Identification :
- ☐ ID Card　☐ Witness
- ☐ Known Personally
- ☐ Driver's License　☐ Passport
- ☐ Others

Service Performed :
- ☐ Jurat　☐ Oath
- ☐ Acknowledgement
- ☐ Others

Witness Name :

Email Address :

Witness Signature :

Address :

Phone No. :

NOTE :

✦ NOTARY LOGBOOK ✦ / 85

Printed Name :

Email Address :

Phone No. :

Address :

Signer's Signature :

Thumb Print :

Document Type :	Date Notarized :	Document Date :	Fee Charged :

ID Number :

Issued By :

Date Issued :	Expiration Date :

Identification :
- ☐ ID Card
- ☐ Known Personally
- ☐ Driver's License
- ☐ Witness
- ☐ Passport
- ☐ Others

Service Performed :
- ☐ Jurat
- ☐ Acknowledgement
- ☐ Oath
- ☐ Others

Witness Name :

Address :

Email Address :

Phone No. :

Witness Signature :

NOTE :

✦ NOTARY LOGBOOK ✦ / 86

Printed Name :

Email Address :

Phone No. :

Address :

Signer's Signature :

Thumb Print :

Document Type :	Date Notarized :	Document Date :	Fee Charged :

ID Number :

Issued By :

Date Issued :	Expiration Date :

Identification :
- ☐ ID Card
- ☐ Known Personally
- ☐ Driver's License
- ☐ Witness
- ☐ Passport
- ☐ Others

Service Performed :
- ☐ Jurat
- ☐ Acknowledgement
- ☐ Oath
- ☐ Others

Witness Name :

Address :

Email Address :

Phone No. :

Witness Signature :

NOTE :

→ NOTARY LOGBOOK ← / 87

Printed Name :	Signer's Signature :	Thumb Print :
Email Address :		
Phone No. :		
Address :		

Document Type :	Date Notarized :	Document Date :	Fee Charged :

ID Number :

Issued By :

Date Issued :	Expiration Date :

Identification :
- ☐ ID Card   ☐ Witness
- ☐ Known Personally
- ☐ Driver's License   ☐ Passport
- ☐ Others

Service Performed :
- ☐ Jurat   ☐ Oath
- ☐ Acknowledgement
- ☐ Others

Witness Name :	Address :
Email Address :	Phone No. :
Witness Signature :	NOTE :

→ NOTARY LOGBOOK ← / 88

Printed Name :	Signer's Signature :	Thumb Print :
Email Address :		
Phone No. :		
Address :		

Document Type :	Date Notarized :	Document Date :	Fee Charged :

ID Number :

Issued By :

Date Issued :	Expiration Date :

Identification :
- ☐ ID Card   ☐ Witness
- ☐ Known Personally
- ☐ Driver's License   ☐ Passport
- ☐ Others

Service Performed :
- ☐ Jurat   ☐ Oath
- ☐ Acknowledgement
- ☐ Others

Witness Name :	Address :
Email Address :	Phone No. :
Witness Signature :	NOTE :

Printed Name :

Email Address :

Phone No. :

Address :

Signer's Signature :

Thumb Print :

Document Type :	Date Notarized :	Document Date :	Fee Charged :

ID Number :

Issued By :

Date Issued :	Expiration Date :

Identification :
- ☐ ID Card   ☐ Witness
- ☐ Known Personally
- ☐ Driver's License   ☐ Passport
- ☐ Others

Service Performed :
- ☐ Jurat   ☐ Oath
- ☐ Acknowledgement
- ☐ Others

Witness Name :

Address :

Email Address :

Phone No. :

Witness Signature :

NOTE :

Printed Name :

Email Address :

Phone No. :

Address :

Signer's Signature :

Thumb Print :

Document Type :	Date Notarized :	Document Date :	Fee Charged :

ID Number :

Issued By :

Date Issued :	Expiration Date :

Identification :
- ☐ ID Card   ☐ Witness
- ☐ Known Personally
- ☐ Driver's License   ☐ Passport
- ☐ Others

Service Performed :
- ☐ Jurat   ☐ Oath
- ☐ Acknowledgement
- ☐ Others

Witness Name :

Address :

Email Address :

Phone No. :

Witness Signature :

NOTE :

⤙ NOTARY LOGBOOK ⤚ / 91

Printed Name :

Email Address :

Phone No. :

Address :

Signer's Signature :

Thumb Print :

Document Type :	Date Notarized :	Document Date :	Fee Charged :

ID Number :

Issued By :

Date Issued : | Expiration Date :

Identification :
- ☐ ID Card
- ☐ Witness
- ☐ Known Personally
- ☐ Driver's License
- ☐ Passport
- ☐ Others

Service Performed :
- ☐ Jurat
- ☐ Oath
- ☐ Acknowledgement
- ☐ Others

Witness Name :

Email Address :

Witness Signature :

Address :

Phone No. :

NOTE :

⤙ NOTARY LOGBOOK ⤚ / 92

Printed Name :

Email Address :

Phone No. :

Address :

Signer's Signature :

Thumb Print :

Document Type :	Date Notarized :	Document Date :	Fee Charged :

ID Number :

Issued By :

Date Issued : | Expiration Date :

Identification :
- ☐ ID Card
- ☐ Witness
- ☐ Known Personally
- ☐ Driver's License
- ☐ Passport
- ☐ Others

Service Performed :
- ☐ Jurat
- ☐ Oath
- ☐ Acknowledgement
- ☐ Others

Witness Name :

Email Address :

Witness Signature :

Address :

Phone No. :

NOTE :

Printed Name :

Email Address :

Phone No. :

Address :

Signer's Signature :

Thumb Print :

Document Type :	Date Notarized :	Document Date :	Fee Charged :

ID Number :

Issued By :

Date Issued :	Expiration Date :

Identification :
- ☐ ID Card   ☐ Witness
- ☐ Known Personally
- ☐ Driver's License   ☐ Passport
- ☐ Others

Service Performed :
- ☐ Jurat   ☐ Oath
- ☐ Acknowledgement
- ☐ Others

Witness Name :

Email Address :

Witness Signature :

Address :

Phone No. :

NOTE :

Printed Name :

Email Address :

Phone No. :

Address :

Signer's Signature :

Thumb Print :

Document Type :	Date Notarized :	Document Date :	Fee Charged :

ID Number :

Issued By :

Date Issued :	Expiration Date :

Identification :
- ☐ ID Card   ☐ Witness
- ☐ Known Personally
- ☐ Driver's License   ☐ Passport
- ☐ Others

Service Performed :
- ☐ Jurat   ☐ Oath
- ☐ Acknowledgement
- ☐ Others

Witness Name :

Email Address :

Witness Signature :

Address :

Phone No. :

NOTE :

Printed Name :

Email Address :

Phone No. :

Address :

Signer's Signature :

Thumb Print :

Document Type :	Date Notarized :	Document Date :	Fee Charged :

ID Number :

Issued By :

Date Issued : Expiration Date :

Identification :
- ☐ ID Card   ☐ Witness
- ☐ Known Personally
- ☐ Driver's License   ☐ Passport
- ☐ Others

Service Performed :
- ☐ Jurat   ☐ Oath
- ☐ Acknowledgement
- ☐ Others

Witness Name :

Address :

Email Address :

Phone No. :

Witness Signature :

NOTE :

Printed Name :

Email Address :

Phone No. :

Address :

Signer's Signature :

Thumb Print :

Document Type :	Date Notarized :	Document Date :	Fee Charged :

ID Number :

Issued By :

Date Issued : Expiration Date :

Identification :
- ☐ ID Card   ☐ Witness
- ☐ Known Personally
- ☐ Driver's License   ☐ Passport
- ☐ Others

Service Performed :
- ☐ Jurat   ☐ Oath
- ☐ Acknowledgement
- ☐ Others

Witness Name :

Address :

Email Address :

Phone No. :

Witness Signature :

NOTE :

Printed Name :

Signer's Signature :

Thumb Print :

Email Address :

Phone No. :

Address :

Document Type :	Date Notarized :	Document Date :	Fee Charged :

ID Number :

Issued By :

Date Issued :	Expiration Date :

Identification :
- ☐ ID Card
- ☐ Witness
- ☐ Known Personally
- ☐ Driver's License
- ☐ Passport
- ☐ Others

Service Performed :
- ☐ Jurat
- ☐ Oath
- ☐ Acknowledgement
- ☐ Others

Witness Name :

Address :

Email Address :

Phone No. :

Witness Signature :

NOTE :

Printed Name :

Signer's Signature :

Thumb Print :

Email Address :

Phone No. :

Address :

Document Type :	Date Notarized :	Document Date :	Fee Charged :

ID Number :

Issued By :

Date Issued :	Expiration Date :

Identification :
- ☐ ID Card
- ☐ Witness
- ☐ Known Personally
- ☐ Driver's License
- ☐ Passport
- ☐ Others

Service Performed :
- ☐ Jurat
- ☐ Oath
- ☐ Acknowledgement
- ☐ Others

Witness Name :

Address :

Email Address :

Phone No. :

Witness Signature :

NOTE :

✦ NOTARY LOGBOOK ✦ / 99

Printed Name :

Email Address :

Phone No. :

Address :

Signer's Signature :

Thumb Print :

Document Type :	Date Notarized :	Document Date :	Fee Charged :

ID Number :

Issued By :

Date Issued : | Expiration Date :

Identification :
- ☐ ID Card
- ☐ Known Personally
- ☐ Driver's License
- ☐ Witness
- ☐ Passport
- ☐ Others

Service Performed :
- ☐ Jurat
- ☐ Acknowledgement
- ☐ Oath
- ☐ Others

Witness Name :

Email Address :

Witness Signature :

Address :

Phone No. :

NOTE :

✦ NOTARY LOGBOOK ✦ / 100

Printed Name :

Email Address :

Phone No. :

Address :

Signer's Signature :

Thumb Print :

Document Type :	Date Notarized :	Document Date :	Fee Charged :

ID Number :

Issued By :

Date Issued : | Expiration Date :

Identification :
- ☐ ID Card
- ☐ Known Personally
- ☐ Driver's License
- ☐ Witness
- ☐ Passport
- ☐ Others

Service Performed :
- ☐ Jurat
- ☐ Acknowledgement
- ☐ Oath
- ☐ Others

Witness Name :

Email Address :

Witness Signature :

Address :

Phone No. :

NOTE :

✦ NOTARY LOGBOOK ✦

Printed Name :

Email Address :

Phone No. :

Address :

Signer's Signature :

Thumb Print :

Document Type :	Date Notarized :	Document Date :	Fee Charged :

ID Number :

Issued By :

Date Issued :	Expiration Date :

Identification :
- ☐ ID Card   ☐ Witness
- ☐ Known Personally
- ☐ Driver's License   ☐ Passport
- ☐ Others

Service Performed :
- ☐ Jurat   ☐ Oath
- ☐ Acknowledgement

☐ Others

Witness Name :

Email Address :

Witness Signature :

Address :

Phone No. :

NOTE :

✦ NOTARY LOGBOOK ✦

Printed Name :

Email Address :

Phone No. :

Address :

Signer's Signature :

Thumb Print :

Document Type :	Date Notarized :	Document Date :	Fee Charged :

ID Number :

Issued By :

Date Issued :	Expiration Date :

Identification :
- ☐ ID Card   ☐ Witness
- ☐ Known Personally
- ☐ Driver's License   ☐ Passport
- ☐ Others

Service Performed :
- ☐ Jurat   ☐ Oath
- ☐ Acknowledgement

☐ Others

Witness Name :

Email Address :

Witness Signature :

Address :

Phone No. :

NOTE :

Printed Name :

Email Address :

Phone No. :

Address :

Signer's Signature :

Thumb Print :

Document Type :	Date Notarized :	Document Date :	Fee Charged :

ID Number :

Issued By :

Date Issued : | Expiration Date :

Identification :
- ☐ ID Card   ☐ Witness
- ☐ Known Personally
- ☐ Driver's License   ☐ Passport
- ☐ Others

Service Performed :
- ☐ Jurat   ☐ Oath
- ☐ Acknowledgement
- ☐ Others

Witness Name :

Email Address :

Witness Signature :

Address :

Phone No. :

NOTE :

Printed Name :

Email Address :

Phone No. :

Address :

Signer's Signature :

Thumb Print :

Document Type :	Date Notarized :	Document Date :	Fee Charged :

ID Number :

Issued By :

Date Issued : | Expiration Date :

Identification :
- ☐ ID Card   ☐ Witness
- ☐ Known Personally
- ☐ Driver's License   ☐ Passport
- ☐ Others

Service Performed :
- ☐ Jurat   ☐ Oath
- ☐ Acknowledgement
- ☐ Others

Witness Name :

Email Address :

Witness Signature :

Address :

Phone No. :

NOTE :

⤞ NOTARY LOGBOOK ⤝ / 105

Printed Name :

Email Address :

Phone No. :

Address :

Signer's Signature :

Thumb Print :

Document Type :	Date Notarized :	Document Date :	Fee Charged :

ID Number :

Issued By :

Date Issued :	Expiration Date :

Identification :
- ☐ ID Card
- ☐ Witness
- ☐ Known Personally
- ☐ Driver's License
- ☐ Passport
- ☐ Others

Service Performed :
- ☐ Jurat
- ☐ Oath
- ☐ Acknowledgement
- ☐ Others

Witness Name :	Address :
Email Address :	Phone No. :
Witness Signature :	NOTE :

⤞ NOTARY LOGBOOK ⤝ / 106

Printed Name :

Email Address :

Phone No. :

Address :

Signer's Signature :

Thumb Print :

Document Type :	Date Notarized :	Document Date :	Fee Charged :

ID Number :

Issued By :

Date Issued :	Expiration Date :

Identification :
- ☐ ID Card
- ☐ Witness
- ☐ Known Personally
- ☐ Driver's License
- ☐ Passport
- ☐ Others

Service Performed :
- ☐ Jurat
- ☐ Oath
- ☐ Acknowledgement
- ☐ Others

Witness Name :	Address :
Email Address :	Phone No. :
Witness Signature :	NOTE :

❖ NOTARY LOGBOOK ❖ / 107

Printed Name :

Email Address :

Phone No. :

Address :

Signer's Signature :

Thumb Print :

Document Type :	Date Notarized :	Document Date :	Fee Charged :

ID Number :

Issued By :

Date Issued :   Expiration Date :

Identification :
- ☐ ID Card
- ☐ Witness
- ☐ Known Personally
- ☐ Driver's License
- ☐ Passport
- ☐ Others

Service Performed :
- ☐ Jurat
- ☐ Oath
- ☐ Acknowledgement
- ☐ Others

Witness Name :

Email Address :

Witness Signature :

Address :

Phone No. :

NOTE :

❖ NOTARY LOGBOOK ❖ / 108

Printed Name :

Email Address :

Phone No. :

Address :

Signer's Signature :

Thumb Print :

Document Type :	Date Notarized :	Document Date :	Fee Charged :

ID Number :

Issued By :

Date Issued :   Expiration Date :

Identification :
- ☐ ID Card
- ☐ Witness
- ☐ Known Personally
- ☐ Driver's License
- ☐ Passport
- ☐ Others

Service Performed :
- ☐ Jurat
- ☐ Oath
- ☐ Acknowledgement
- ☐ Others

Witness Name :

Email Address :

Witness Signature :

Address :

Phone No. :

NOTE :

✦ NOTARY LOGBOOK ✦ / 109

Printed Name :	**Signer's Signature :**	**Thumb Print :**
Email Address :		
Phone No. :		
Address :		

Document Type :	Date Notarized :	Document Date :	Fee Charged :

ID Number :	**Identification :**	**Service Performed :**
	☐ ID Card ☐ Witness	☐ Jurat ☐ Oath
Issued By :	☐ Known Personally	☐ Acknowledgement
	☐ Driver's License ☐ Passport	
Date Issued : **Expiration Date :**	☐ Others	☐ Others

Witness Name :	**Address :**
Email Address :	**Phone No. :**
Witness Signature :	**NOTE :**

✦ NOTARY LOGBOOK ✦ / 110

Printed Name :	**Signer's Signature :**	**Thumb Print :**
Email Address :		
Phone No. :		
Address :		

Document Type :	Date Notarized :	Document Date :	Fee Charged :

ID Number :	**Identification :**	**Service Performed :**
	☐ ID Card ☐ Witness	☐ Jurat ☐ Oath
Issued By :	☐ Known Personally	☐ Acknowledgement
	☐ Driver's License ☐ Passport	
Date Issued : **Expiration Date :**	☐ Others	☐ Others

Witness Name :	**Address :**
Email Address :	**Phone No. :**
Witness Signature :	**NOTE :**

⤜ NOTARY LOGBOOK ⤛ / 111

Printed Name :	Signer's Signature :	Thumb Print :
Email Address :		
Phone No. :		
Address :		

Document Type :	Date Notarized :	Document Date :	Fee Charged :

ID Number :	Identification :	Service Performed :
	☐ ID Card ☐ Witness	☐ Jurat ☐ Oath
Issued By :	☐ Known Personally	☐ Acknowledgement
	☐ Driver's License ☐ Passport	
Date Issued : Expiration Date :	☐ Others	☐ Others

Witness Name :	Address :
Email Address :	Phone No. :
Witness Signature :	NOTE :

⤜ NOTARY LOGBOOK ⤛ / 112

Printed Name :	Signer's Signature :	Thumb Print :
Email Address :		
Phone No. :		
Address :		

Document Type :	Date Notarized :	Document Date :	Fee Charged :

ID Number :	Identification :	Service Performed :
	☐ ID Card ☐ Witness	☐ Jurat ☐ Oath
Issued By :	☐ Known Personally	☐ Acknowledgement
	☐ Driver's License ☐ Passport	
Date Issued : Expiration Date :	☐ Others	☐ Others

Witness Name :	Address :
Email Address :	Phone No. :
Witness Signature :	NOTE :

Printed Name :

Signer's Signature :

Thumb Print :

Email Address :

Phone No. :

Address :

Document Type :	Date Notarized :	Document Date :	Fee Charged :

ID Number :

Issued By :

Date Issued : Expiration Date :

Identification :

☐ ID Card   ☐ Witness
☐ Known Personally
☐ Driver's License   ☐ Passport
          ☐ Others

Service Performed :

☐ Jurat   ☐ Oath
☐ Acknowledgement

       ☐ Others

Witness Name :

Address :

Email Address :

Phone No. :

Witness Signature :

NOTE :

Printed Name :

Signer's Signature :

Thumb Print :

Email Address :

Phone No. :

Address :

Document Type :	Date Notarized :	Document Date :	Fee Charged :

ID Number :

Issued By :

Date Issued : Expiration Date :

Identification :

☐ ID Card   ☐ Witness
☐ Known Personally
☐ Driver's License   ☐ Passport
          ☐ Others

Service Performed :

☐ Jurat   ☐ Oath
☐ Acknowledgement

       ☐ Others

Witness Name :

Address :

Email Address :

Phone No. :

Witness Signature :

NOTE :

Printed Name :

Signer's Signature :

Thumb Print :

Email Address :

Phone No. :

Address :

| Document Type : | Date Notarized : | Document Date : | Fee Charged : |

ID Number :

Identification :
- ☐ ID Card ☐ Witness
- ☐ Known Personally
- ☐ Driver's License ☐ Passport
- ☐ Others

Service Performed :
- ☐ Jurat ☐ Oath
- ☐ Acknowledgement
- ☐ Others

Issued By :

Date Issued :   Expiration Date :

Witness Name :

Address :

Email Address :

Phone No. :

Witness Signature :

NOTE :

Printed Name :

Signer's Signature :

Thumb Print :

Email Address :

Phone No. :

Address :

| Document Type : | Date Notarized : | Document Date : | Fee Charged : |

ID Number :

Identification :
- ☐ ID Card ☐ Witness
- ☐ Known Personally
- ☐ Driver's License ☐ Passport
- ☐ Others

Service Performed :
- ☐ Jurat ☐ Oath
- ☐ Acknowledgement
- ☐ Others

Issued By :

Date Issued :   Expiration Date :

Witness Name :

Address :

Email Address :

Phone No. :

Witness Signature :

NOTE :

✦ NOTARY LOGBOOK ✦ / 117

Printed Name :

Email Adress :

Phone No. :

Address :

Signer's Signature :

Thumb Print :

Document Type :	Date Notarized :	Document Date :	Fee Charged :

ID Number :

Issued By :

Date Issued :	Expiration Date :

Identification :
- ☐ ID Card
- ☐ Known Personally
- ☐ Driver's License
- ☐ Witness
- ☐ Passport
- ☐ Others

Service Performed :
- ☐ Jurat
- ☐ Oath
- ☐ Acknowledgement
- ☐ Others

Witness Name :

Email Address :

Witness Signature :

Address :

Phone No. :

NOTE :

✦ NOTARY LOGBOOK ✦ / 118

Printed Name :

Email Address :

Phone No. :

Address :

Signer's Signature :

Thumb Print :

Document Type :	Date Notarized :	Document Date :	Fee Charged :

ID Number :

Issued By :

Date Issued :	Expiration Date :

Identification :
- ☐ ID Card
- ☐ Known Personally
- ☐ Driver's License
- ☐ Witness
- ☐ Passport
- ☐ Others

Service Performed :
- ☐ Jurat
- ☐ Oath
- ☐ Acknowledgement
- ☐ Others

Witness Name :

Email Address :

Witness Signature :

Address :

Phone No. :

NOTE :

Printed Name :

Email Address :

Phone No. :

Address :

Signer's Signature :

Thumb Print :

Document Type :	Date Notarized :	Document Date :	Fee Charged :

ID Number :

Issued By :

Date Issued : | **Expiration Date :**

Identification :
- ☐ ID Card ☐ Witness
- ☐ Known Personally
- ☐ Driver's License ☐ Passport
- ☐ Others

Service Performed :
- ☐ Jurat ☐ Oath
- ☐ Acknowledgement
- ☐ Others

Witness Name :

Email Address :

Witness Signature :

Address :

Phone No. :

NOTE :

Printed Name :

Email Address :

Phone No. :

Address :

Signer's Signature :

Thumb Print :

Document Type :	Date Notarized :	Document Date :	Fee Charged :

ID Number :

Issued By :

Date Issued : | **Expiration Date :**

Identification :
- ☐ ID Card ☐ Witness
- ☐ Known Personally
- ☐ Driver's License ☐ Passport
- ☐ Others

Service Performed :
- ☐ Jurat ☐ Oath
- ☐ Acknowledgement
- ☐ Others

Witness Name :

Email Address :

Witness Signature :

Address :

Phone No. :

NOTE :

⤞ NOTARY LOGBOOK ⤝

Printed Name :

Signer's Signature :

Thumb Print :

Email Address :

Phone No. :

Address :

Document Type :	Date Notarized :	Document Date :	Fee Charged :

ID Number :

Identification :
- ☐ ID Card ☐ Witness
- ☐ Known Personally
- ☐ Driver's License ☐ Passport
- ☐ Others

Service Performed :
- ☐ Jurat ☐ Oath
- ☐ Acknowledgement
- ☐ Others

Issued By :

Date Issued :	Expiration Date :

Witness Name :

Address :

Email Address :

Phone No. :

Witness Signature :

NOTE :

⤞ NOTARY LOGBOOK ⤝

Printed Name :

Signer's Signature :

Thumb Print :

Email Address :

Phone No. :

Address :

Document Type :	Date Notarized :	Document Date :	Fee Charged :

ID Number :

Identification :
- ☐ ID Card ☐ Witness
- ☐ Known Personally
- ☐ Driver's License ☐ Passport
- ☐ Others

Service Performed :
- ☐ Jurat ☐ Oath
- ☐ Acknowledgement
- ☐ Others

Issued By :

Date Issued :	Expiration Date :

Witness Name :

Address :

Email Address :

Phone No. :

Witness Signature :

NOTE :

⤜ NOTARY LOGBOOK ⤛ / 123

Printed Name :	Signer's Signature :	Thumb Print :
Email Address :		
Phone No. :		
Address :		

Document Type :	Date Notarized :	Document Date :	Fee Charged :

ID Number :	Identification :	Service Performed :
	☐ ID Card ☐ Witness	☐ Jurat ☐ Oath
Issued By :	☐ Known Personally	☐ Acknowledgement
	☐ Driver's License ☐ Passport	
Date Issued : Expiration Date :	☐ Others	☐ Others

Witness Name :	Address :
Email Address :	Phone No. :
Witness Signature :	NOTE :

⤜ NOTARY LOGBOOK ⤛ / 124

Printed Name :	Signer's Signature :	Thumb Print :
Email Address :		
Phone No. :		
Address :		

Document Type :	Date Notarized :	Document Date :	Fee Charged :

ID Number :	Identification :	Service Performed :
	☐ ID Card ☐ Witness	☐ Jurat ☐ Oath
Issued By :	☐ Known Personally	☐ Acknowledgement
	☐ Driver's License ☐ Passport	
Date Issued : Expiration Date :	☐ Others	☐ Others

Witness Name :	Address :
Email Address :	Phone No. :
Witness Signature :	NOTE :

⤜ NOTARY LOGBOOK ⤛

Printed Name :

Email Address :

Phone No. :

Address :

Signer's Signature :

Thumb Print :

Document Type :	Date Notarized :	Document Date :	Fee Charged :

ID Number :

Issued By :

Date Issued :

Expiration Date :

Identification :
- ☐ ID Card
- ☐ Known Personally
- ☐ Driver's License
- ☐ Witness
- ☐ Passport
- ☐ Others

Service Performed :
- ☐ Jurat
- ☐ Acknowledgement
- ☐ Oath
- ☐ Others

Witness Name :

Address :

Email Address :

Phone No. :

Witness Signature :

NOTE :

⤜ NOTARY LOGBOOK ⤛

Printed Name :

Email Address :

Phone No. :

Address :

Signer's Signature :

Thumb Print :

Document Type :	Date Notarized :	Document Date :	Fee Charged :

ID Number :

Issued By :

Date Issued :

Expiration Date :

Identification :
- ☐ ID Card
- ☐ Known Personally
- ☐ Driver's License
- ☐ Witness
- ☐ Passport
- ☐ Others

Service Performed :
- ☐ Jurat
- ☐ Acknowledgement
- ☐ Oath
- ☐ Others

Witness Name :

Address :

Email Address :

Phone No. :

Witness Signature :

NOTE :

✦ NOTARY LOGBOOK ✦ / 127

Printed Name :

Email Address :

Phone No. :

Address :

Signer's Signature :

Thumb Print :

Document Type :	Date Notarized :	Document Date :	Fee Charged :

ID Number :

Issued By :

Date Issued : | **Expiration Date :**

Identification :
- ☐ ID Card ☐ Witness
- ☐ Known Personally
- ☐ Driver's License ☐ Passport
- ☐ Others

Service Performed :
- ☐ Jurat ☐ Oath
- ☐ Acknowledgement
- ☐ Others

Witness Name :

Email Address :

Witness Signature :

Address :

Phone No. :

NOTE :

✦ NOTARY LOGBOOK ✦ / 128

Printed Name :

Email Address :

Phone No. :

Address :

Signer's Signature :

Thumb Print :

Document Type :	Date Notarized :	Document Date :	Fee Charged :

ID Number :

Issued By :

Date Issued : | **Expiration Date :**

Identification :
- ☐ ID Card ☐ Witness
- ☐ Known Personally
- ☐ Driver's License ☐ Passport
- ☐ Others

Service Performed :
- ☐ Jurat ☐ Oath
- ☐ Acknowledgement
- ☐ Others

Witness Name :

Email Address :

Witness Signature :

Address :

Phone No. :

NOTE :

✦ NOTARY LOGBOOK ✦ 129

Printed Name :

Signer's Signature :

Thumb Print :

Email Address :

Phone No. :

Address :

Document Type :	Date Notarized :	Document Date :	Fee Charged :

ID Number :

Issued By :

Date Issued :	Expiration Date :

Identification :
- ☐ ID Card   ☐ Witness
- ☐ Known Personally
- ☐ Driver's License ☐ Passport
- ☐ Others

Service Performed :
- ☐ Jurat   ☐ Oath
- ☐ Acknowledgement
- ☐ Others

Witness Name :

Address :

Email Address :

Phone No. :

Witness Signature :

NOTE :

✦ NOTARY LOGBOOK ✦ 130

Printed Name :

Signer's Signature :

Thumb Print :

Email Address :

Phone No. :

Address :

Document Type :	Date Notarized :	Document Date :	Fee Charged :

ID Number :

Issued By :

Date Issued :	Expiration Date :

Identification :
- ☐ ID Card   ☐ Witness
- ☐ Known Personally
- ☐ Driver's License ☐ Passport
- ☐ Others

Service Performed :
- ☐ Jurat   ☐ Oath
- ☐ Acknowledgement
- ☐ Others

Witness Name :

Address :

Email Address :

Phone No. :

Witness Signature :

NOTE :

Printed Name :

Signer's Signature :

Thumb Print :

Email Address :

Phone No. :

Address :

Document Type :	Date Notarized :	Document Date :	Fee Charged :

ID Number :

Issued By :

Date Issued :   Expiration Date :

Identification :
- ☐ ID Card   ☐ Witness
- ☐ Known Personally
- ☐ Driver's License   ☐ Passport
- ☐ Others

Service Performed :
- ☐ Jurat   ☐ Oath
- ☐ Acknowledgement
- ☐ Others

Witness Name :

Address :

Email Address :

Phone No. :

Witness Signature :

NOTE :

➤ NOTARY LOGBOOK ➤ / 132

Printed Name :

Signer's Signature :

Thumb Print :

Email Address :

Phone No. :

Address :

Document Type :	Date Notarized :	Document Date :	Fee Charged :

ID Number :

Issued By :

Date Issued :   Expiration Date :

Identification :
- ☐ ID Card   ☐ Witness
- ☐ Known Personally
- ☐ Driver's License   ☐ Passport
- ☐ Others

Service Performed :
- ☐ Jurat   ☐ Oath
- ☐ Acknowledgement
- ☐ Others

Witness Name :

Address :

Email Address :

Phone No. :

Witness Signature :

NOTE :

Printed Name :	Signer's Signature :	Thumb Print :
Email Address :		
Phone No. :		
Address :		

Document Type :	Date Notarized :	Document Date :	Fee Charged :

ID Number :	Identification :	Service Performed :
	☐ ID Card ☐ Witness	☐ Jurat ☐ Oath
	☐ Known Personally	☐ Acknowledgement
Issued By :	☐ Driver's License ☐ Passport	
Date Issued : Expiration Date :	☐ Others	☐ Others

Witness Name :	Address :
Email Address :	Phone No. :
Witness Signature :	NOTE :

Printed Name :	Signer's Signature :	Thumb Print :
Email Address :		
Phone No. :		
Address :		

Document Type :	Date Notarized :	Document Date :	Fee Charged :

ID Number :	Identification :	Service Performed :
	☐ ID Card ☐ Witness	☐ Jurat ☐ Oath
	☐ Known Personally	☐ Acknowledgement
Issued By :	☐ Driver's License ☐ Passport	
Date Issued : Expiration Date :	☐ Others	☐ Others

Witness Name :	Address :
Email Address :	Phone No. :
Witness Signature :	NOTE :

Printed Name :

Signer's Signature :

Thumb Print :

Email Address :

Phone No. :

Address :

Document Type :	Date Notarized :	Document Date :	Fee Charged :

ID Number :

Issued By :

Date Issued : | Expiration Date :

Identification :
- ☐ ID Card   ☐ Witness
- ☐ Known Personally
- ☐ Driver's License   ☐ Passport
- ☐ Others

Service Performed :
- ☐ Jurat   ☐ Oath
- ☐ Acknowledgement
- ☐ Others

Witness Name : | Address :

Email Address : | Phone No. :

Witness Signature : | NOTE :

Printed Name :

Signer's Signature :

Thumb Print :

Email Address :

Phone No. :

Address :

Document Type :	Date Notarized :	Document Date :	Fee Charged :

ID Number :

Issued By :

Date Issued : | Expiration Date :

Identification :
- ☐ ID Card   ☐ Witness
- ☐ Known Personally
- ☐ Driver's License   ☐ Passport
- ☐ Others

Service Performed :
- ☐ Jurat   ☐ Oath
- ☐ Acknowledgement
- ☐ Others

Witness Name : | Address :

Email Address : | Phone No. :

Witness Signature : | NOTE :

Printed Name :

Email Address :

Phone No. :

Address :

Signer's Signature :

Thumb Print :

Document Type :	Date Notarized :	Document Date :	Fee Charged :

ID Number :

Issued By :

Date Issued :	Expiration Date :

Identification :
- ☐ ID Card   ☐ Witness
- ☐ Known Personally
- ☐ Driver's License   ☐ Passport
- ☐ Others

Service Performed :
- ☐ Jurat   ☐ Oath
- ☐ Acknowledgement
- ☐ Others

Witness Name :

Address :

Email Address :

Phone No. :

Witness Signature :

NOTE :

Printed Name :

Email Address :

Phone No. :

Address :

Signer's Signature :

Thumb Print :

Document Type :	Date Notarized :	Document Date :	Fee Charged :

ID Number :

Issued By :

Date Issued :	Expiration Date :

Identification :
- ☐ ID Card   ☐ Witness
- ☐ Known Personally
- ☐ Driver's License   ☐ Passport
- ☐ Others

Service Performed :
- ☐ Jurat   ☐ Oath
- ☐ Acknowledgement
- ☐ Others

Witness Name :

Address :

Email Address :

Phone No. :

Witness Signature :

NOTE :

✦ NOTARY LOGBOOK ✦ / 139

Printed Name :

Email Address :

Phone No. :

Address :

Signer's Signature :

Thumb Print :

Document Type :	Date Notarized :	Document Date :	Fee Charged :

ID Number :

Issued By :

Date Issued :   Expiration Date :

Identification :
- ☐ ID Card   ☐ Witness
- ☐ Known Personally
- ☐ Driver's License ☐ Passport
- ☐ Others

Service Performed :
- ☐ Jurat   ☐ Oath
- ☐ Acknowledgement
- ☐ Others

Witness Name :

Email Address :

Witness Signature :

Address :

Phone No. :

NOTE :

✦ NOTARY LOGBOOK ✦ / 140

Printed Name :

Email Address :

Phone No. :

Address :

Signer's Signature :

Thumb Print :

Document Type :	Date Notarized :	Document Date :	Fee Charged :

ID Number :

Issued By :

Date Issued :   Expiration Date :

Identification :
- ☐ ID Card   ☐ Witness
- ☐ Known Personally
- ☐ Driver's License ☐ Passport
- ☐ Others

Service Performed :
- ☐ Jurat   ☐ Oath
- ☐ Acknowledgement
- ☐ Others

Witness Name :

Email Address :

Witness Signature :

Address :

Phone No. :

NOTE :

⇥ NOTARY LOGBOOK ⇤ / 141

Printed Name :

Email Address :

Phone No. :

Address :

Signer's Signature :

Thumb Print :

Document Type :	Date Notarized :	Document Date :	Fee Charged :

ID Number :

Issued By :

Date Issued :	Expiration Date :

Identification :
- ☐ ID Card   ☐ Witness
- ☐ Known Personally
- ☐ Driver's License   ☐ Passport
- ☐ Others

Service Performed :
- ☐ Jurat   ☐ Oath
- ☐ Acknowledgement
- ☐ Others

Witness Name :

Email Adress :

Witness Signature :

Address :

Phone No. :

NOTE :

⇥ NOTARY LOGBOOK ⇤ / 142

Printed Name :

Email Address :

Phone No. :

Address :

Signer's Signature :

Thumb Print :

Document Type :	Date Notarized :	Document Date :	Fee Charged :

ID Number :

Issued By :

Date Issued :	Expiration Date :

Identification :
- ☐ ID Card   ☐ Witness
- ☐ Known Personally
- ☐ Driver's License   ☐ Passport
- ☐ Others

Service Performed :
- ☐ Jurat   ☐ Oath
- ☐ Acknowledgement
- ☐ Others

Witness Name :

Email Address :

Witness Signature :

Address :

Phone No. :

NOTE :

✦ NOTARY LOGBOOK ✦ / 143

Printed Name :

Email Address :

Phone No. :

Address :

Signer's Signature :

Thumb Print :

Document Type :	Date Notarized :	Document Date :	Fee Charged :

ID Number :

Issued By :

Date Issued :	Expiration Date :

Identification :
- ☐ ID Card   ☐ Witness
- ☐ Known Personally
- ☐ Driver's License   ☐ Passport
- ☐ Others

Service Performed :
- ☐ Jurat   ☐ Oath
- ☐ Acknowledgement
- ☐ Others

Witness Name :

Address :

Email Address :

Phone No. :

Witness Signature :

NOTE :

✦ NOTARY LOGBOOK ✦ / 144

Printed Name :

Email Address :

Phone No. :

Address :

Signer's Signature :

Thumb Print :

Document Type :	Date Notarized :	Document Date :	Fee Charged :

ID Number :

Issued By :

Date Issued :	Expiration Date :

Identification :
- ☐ ID Card   ☐ Witness
- ☐ Known Personally
- ☐ Driver's License   ☐ Passport
- ☐ Others

Service Performed :
- ☐ Jurat   ☐ Oath
- ☐ Acknowledgement
- ☐ Others

Witness Name :

Address :

Email Address :

Phone No. :

Witness Signature :

NOTE :

☙ NOTARY LOGBOOK ☙ / 145

Printed Name :	Signer's Signature :	Thumb Print :
Email Address :		
Phone No. :		
Address :		

Document Type :	Date Notarized :	Document Date :	Fee Charged :

ID Number :	Identification :	Service Performed :
	☐ ID Card ☐ Witness	☐ Jurat ☐ Oath
Issued By :	☐ Known Personally	☐ Acknowledgement
Date Issued : Expiration Date :	☐ Driver's License ☐ Passport	
	☐ Others	☐ Others

Witness Name :	Address :
Email Address :	Phone No. :
Witness Signature :	NOTE :

☙ NOTARY LOGBOOK ☙ / 146

Printed Name :	Signer's Signature :	Thumb Print :
Email Address :		
Phone No. :		
Address :		

Document Type :	Date Notarized :	Document Date :	Fee Charged :

ID Number :	Identification :	Service Performed :
	☐ ID Card ☐ Witness	☐ Jurat ☐ Oath
Issued By :	☐ Known Personally	☐ Acknowledgement
Date Issued : Expiration Date :	☐ Driver's License ☐ Passport	
	☐ Others	☐ Others

Witness Name :	Address :
Email Address :	Phone No. :
Witness Signature :	NOTE :

⇥ NOTARY LOGBOOK ⇤ / 147

Printed Name :

Email Address :

Phone No. :

Address :

Signer's Signature :

Thumb Print :

Document Type :	Date Notarized :	Document Date :	Fee Charged :

ID Number :

Issued By :

Date Issued :   Expiration Date :

Identification :
- ☐ ID Card   ☐ Witness
- ☐ Known Personally
- ☐ Driver's License   ☐ Passport
- ☐ Others
- - - - - - - - - - - - - - - -

Service Performed :
- ☐ Jurat   ☐ Oath
- ☐ Acknowledgement
- ☐ Others
- - - - - - - - - - - - - - - -

Witness Name :	Address :
Email Address :	Phone No. :
Witness Signature :	NOTE : -

⇥ NOTARY LOGBOOK ⇤ / 148

Printed Name :

Email Address :

Phone No. :

Address :

Signer's Signature :

Thumb Print :

Document Type :	Date Notarized :	Document Date :	Fee Charged :

ID Number :

Issued By :

Date Issued :   Expiration Date :

Identification :
- ☐ ID Card   ☐ Witness
- ☐ Known Personally
- ☐ Driver's License   ☐ Passport
- ☐ Others
- - - - - - - - - - - - - - - -

Service Performed :
- ☐ Jurat   ☐ Oath
- ☐ Acknowledgement
- ☐ Others
- - - - - - - - - - - - - - - -

Witness Name :	Address :
Email Address :	Phone No. :
Witness Signature :	NOTE : -

✦ NOTARY LOGBOOK ✦ / 149

Printed Name :

Email Address :

Phone No. :

Address :

Signer's Signature :

Thumb Print :

Document Type :	Date Notarized :	Document Date :	Fee Charged :

ID Number :

Issued By :

Date Issued :	Expiration Date :

Identification :
- ☐ ID Card
- ☐ Known Personally
- ☐ Driver's License
- ☐ Witness
- ☐ Passport
- ☐ Others

Service Performed :
- ☐ Jurat
- ☐ Oath
- ☐ Acknowledgement
- ☐ Others

Witness Name :

Email Address :

Witness Signature :

Address :

Phone No. :

NOTE :

✦ NOTARY LOGBOOK ✦ / 150

Printed Name :

Email Address :

Phone No. :

Address :

Signer's Signature :

Thumb Print :

Document Type :	Date Notarized :	Document Date :	Fee Charged :

ID Number :

Issued By :

Date Issued :	Expiration Date :

Identification :
- ☐ ID Card
- ☐ Known Personally
- ☐ Driver's License
- ☐ Witness
- ☐ Passport
- ☐ Others

Service Performed :
- ☐ Jurat
- ☐ Oath
- ☐ Acknowledgement
- ☐ Others

Witness Name :

Email Address :

Witness Signature :

Address :

Phone No. :

NOTE :

Printed Name :

Email Address :

Phone No. :

Address :

Signer's Signature :

Thumb Print :

Document Type :	Date Notarized :	Document Date :	Fee Charged :

ID Number :

Issued By :

Date Issued :   Expiration Date :

Identification :

☐ ID Card   ☐ Witness
☐ Known Personally
☐ Driver's License   ☐ Passport
☐ Others

Service Performed :

☐ Jurat   ☐ Oath
☐ Acknowledgement

☐ Others

Witness Name :   Address :

Email Address :   Phone No. :

Witness Signature :   NOTE :

Printed Name :

Email Address :

Phone No. :

Address :

Signer's Signature :

Thumb Print :

Document Type :	Date Notarized :	Document Date :	Fee Charged :

ID Number :

Issued By :

Date Issued :   Expiration Date :

Identification :

☐ ID Card   ☐ Witness
☐ Known Personally
☐ Driver's License   ☐ Passport
☐ Others

Service Performed :

☐ Jurat   ☐ Oath
☐ Acknowledgement

☐ Others

Witness Name :   Address :

Email Address :   Phone No. :

Witness Signature :   NOTE :

⤙ NOTARY LOGBOOK ⤚ / 153

Printed Name :

Email Address :

Phone No. :

Address :

Signer's Signature :

Thumb Print :

Document Type :	Date Notarized :	Document Date :	Fee Charged :

ID Number :

Issued By :

Date Issued :

Expiration Date :

Identification :
- ☐ ID Card
- ☐ Known Personally
- ☐ Driver's License
- ☐ Witness
- ☐ Passport
- ☐ Others

Service Performed :
- ☐ Jurat
- ☐ Oath
- ☐ Acknowledgement
- ☐ Others

Witness Name :

Email Address :

Witness Signature :

Address :

Phone No. :

NOTE :

⤙ NOTARY LOGBOOK ⤚ / 154

Printed Name :

Email Address :

Phone No. :

Address :

Signer's Signature :

Thumb Print :

Document Type :	Date Notarized :	Document Date :	Fee Charged :

ID Number :

Issued By :

Date Issued :

Expiration Date :

Identification :
- ☐ ID Card
- ☐ Known Personally
- ☐ Driver's License
- ☐ Witness
- ☐ Passport
- ☐ Others

Service Performed :
- ☐ Jurat
- ☐ Oath
- ☐ Acknowledgement
- ☐ Others

Witness Name :

Email Address :

Witness Signature :

Address :

Phone No. :

NOTE :

✦ NOTARY LOGBOOK ✦ 155

Printed Name :

Email Address :

Phone No. :

Address :

Signer's Signature :

Thumb Print :

Document Type :	Date Notarized :	Document Date :	Fee Charged :

ID Number :

Issued By :

Date Issued :

Expiration Date :

Identification :
- ☐ ID Card
- ☐ Known Personally
- ☐ Driver's License
- ☐ Witness
- ☐ Passport
- ☐ Others

Service Performed :
- ☐ Jurat
- ☐ Acknowledgement
- ☐ Oath
- ☐ Others

Witness Name :

Address :

Email Address :

Phone No. :

Witness Signature :

NOTE :

✦ NOTARY LOGBOOK ✦ 156

Printed Name :

Email Address :

Phone No. :

Address :

Signer's Signature :

Thumb Print :

Document Type :	Date Notarized :	Document Date :	Fee Charged :

ID Number :

Issued By :

Date Issued :

Expiration Date :

Identification :
- ☐ ID Card
- ☐ Known Personally
- ☐ Driver's License
- ☐ Witness
- ☐ Passport
- ☐ Others

Service Performed :
- ☐ Jurat
- ☐ Acknowledgement
- ☐ Oath
- ☐ Others

Witness Name :

Address :

Email Address :

Phone No. :

Witness Signature :

NOTE :

↠ NOTARY LOGBOOK ↞ / 157

Printed Name :

Email Address :

Phone No. :

Address :

Signer's Signature :

Thumb Print :

Document Type :	Date Notarized :	Document Date :	Fee Charged :

ID Number :

Issued By :

Date Issued :	Expiration Date :

Identification :
- ☐ ID Card   ☐ Witness
- ☐ Known Personally
- ☐ Driver's License ☐ Passport
- ☐ Others

Service Performed :
- ☐ Jurat   ☐ Oath
- ☐ Acknowledgement
- ☐ Others

Witness Name :	Address :
Email Address :	Phone No. :
Witness Signature :	NOTE :

↠ NOTARY LOGBOOK ↞ / 158

Printed Name :

Email Address :

Phone No. :

Address :

Signer's Signature :

Thumb Print :

Document Type :	Date Notarized :	Document Date :	Fee Charged :

ID Number :

Issued By :

Date Issued :	Expiration Date :

Identification :
- ☐ ID Card   ☐ Witness
- ☐ Known Personally
- ☐ Driver's License ☐ Passport
- ☐ Others

Service Performed :
- ☐ Jurat   ☐ Oath
- ☐ Acknowledgement
- ☐ Others

Witness Name :	Address :
Email Address :	Phone No. :
Witness Signature :	NOTE :

Printed Name :

Signer's Signature :

Thumb Print :

Email Address :

Phone No. :

Address :

| Document Type : | Date Notarized : | Document Date : | Fee Charged : |

ID Number :

Issued By :

Date Issued : | Expiration Date :

Identification :
- ☐ ID Card   ☐ Witness
- ☐ Known Personally
- ☐ Driver's License   ☐ Passport
- ☐ Others

Service Performed :
- ☐ Jurat   ☐ Oath
- ☐ Acknowledgement
- ☐ Others

Witness Name :

Address :

Email Address :

Phone No. :

Witness Signature :

NOTE :

Printed Name :

Signer's Signature :

Thumb Print :

Email Address :

Phone No. :

Address :

| Document Type : | Date Notarized : | Document Date : | Fee Charged : |

ID Number :

Issued By :

Date Issued : | Expiration Date :

Identification :
- ☐ ID Card   ☐ Witness
- ☐ Known Personally
- ☐ Driver's License   ☐ Passport
- ☐ Others

Service Performed :
- ☐ Jurat   ☐ Oath
- ☐ Acknowledgement
- ☐ Others

Witness Name :

Address :

Email Address :

Phone No. :

Witness Signature :

NOTE :

Printed Name :

Email Address :

Phone No. :

Address :

Signer's Signature :

Thumb Print :

Document Type :	Date Notarized :	Document Date :	Fee Charged :

ID Number :

Issued By :

Date Issued :　Expiration Date :

Identification :
- ☐ ID Card　☐ Witness
- ☐ Known Personally
- ☐ Driver's License　☐ Passport
- ☐ Others

Service Performed :
- ☐ Jurat　☐ Oath
- ☐ Acknowledgement
- ☐ Others

Witness Name :

Email Address :

Witness Signature :

Address :

Phone No. :

NOTE :

Printed Name :

Email Address :

Phone No. :

Address :

Signer's Signature :

Thumb Print :

Document Type :	Date Notarized :	Document Date :	Fee Charged :

ID Number :

Issued By :

Date Issued :　Expiration Date :

Identification :
- ☐ ID Card　☐ Witness
- ☐ Known Personally
- ☐ Driver's License　☐ Passport
- ☐ Others

Service Performed :
- ☐ Jurat　☐ Oath
- ☐ Acknowledgement
- ☐ Others

Witness Name :

Email Address :

Witness Signature :

Address :

Phone No. :

NOTE :

Printed Name :

Signer's Signature :

Thumb Print :

Email Address :

Phone No. :

Address :

Document Type :	Date Notarized :	Document Date :	Fee Charged :

ID Number :

Issued By :

Date Issued :   Expiration Date :

Identification :

☐ ID Card   ☐ Witness
☐ Known Personally
☐ Driver's License   ☐ Passport
          ☐ Others

Service Performed :

☐ Jurat   ☐ Oath
☐ Acknowledgement

          ☐ Others

Witness Name :

Address :

Email Address :

Phone No. :

Witness Signature :

NOTE :

Printed Name :

Signer's Signature :

Thumb Print :

Email Address :

Phone No. :

Address :

Document Type :	Date Notarized :	Document Date :	Fee Charged :

ID Number :

Issued By :

Date Issued :   Expiration Date :

Identification :

☐ ID Card   ☐ Witness
☐ Known Personally
☐ Driver's License   ☐ Passport
          ☐ Others

Service Performed :

☐ Jurat   ☐ Oath
☐ Acknowledgement

          ☐ Others

Witness Name :

Address :

Email Address :

Phone No. :

Witness Signature :

NOTE :

✦ NOTARY LOGBOOK ✦

Printed Name :

Signer's Signature :

Thumb Print :

Email Address :

Phone No. :

Address :

Document Type :	Date Notarized :	Document Date :	Fee Charged :

ID Number :

Issued By :

Date Issued :	Expiration Date :

Identification :
- ☐ ID Card
- ☐ Known Personally
- ☐ Driver's License
- ☐ Witness
- ☐ Passport
- ☐ Others

Service Performed :
- ☐ Jurat
- ☐ Oath
- ☐ Acknowledgement
- ☐ Others

Witness Name :

Address :

Email Address :

Phone No. :

Witness Signature :

NOTE :

✦ NOTARY LOGBOOK ✦

Printed Name :

Signer's Signature :

Thumb Print :

Email Address :

Phone No. :

Address :

Document Type :	Date Notarized :	Document Date :	Fee Charged :

ID Number :

Issued By :

Date Issued :	Expiration Date :

Identification :
- ☐ ID Card
- ☐ Known Personally
- ☐ Driver's License
- ☐ Witness
- ☐ Passport
- ☐ Others

Service Performed :
- ☐ Jurat
- ☐ Oath
- ☐ Acknowledgement
- ☐ Others

Witness Name :

Address :

Email Address :

Phone No. :

Witness Signature :

NOTE :

Printed Name :

Email Address :

Phone No. :

Address :

Signer's Signature :

Thumb Print :

Document Type :	Date Notarized :	Document Date :	Fee Charged :

ID Number :

Issued By :

Date Issued :	Expiration Date :

Identification :
- ☐ ID Card
- ☐ Witness
- ☐ Known Personally
- ☐ Driver's License
- ☐ Passport
- ☐ Others

Service Performed :
- ☐ Jurat
- ☐ Oath
- ☐ Acknowledgement
- ☐ Others

Witness Name :

Address :

Email Address :

Phone No. :

Witness Signature :

NOTE :

Printed Name :

Email Address :

Phone No. :

Address :

Signer's Signature :

Thumb Print :

Document Type :	Date Notarized :	Document Date :	Fee Charged :

ID Number :

Issued By :

Date Issued :	Expiration Date :

Identification :
- ☐ ID Card
- ☐ Witness
- ☐ Known Personally
- ☐ Driver's License
- ☐ Passport
- ☐ Others

Service Performed :
- ☐ Jurat
- ☐ Oath
- ☐ Acknowledgement
- ☐ Others

Witness Name :

Address :

Email Address :

Phone No. :

Witness Signature :

NOTE :

❖ NOTARY LOGBOOK ❖ / 169

Printed Name :	Signer's Signature :	Thumb Print :
Email Address :		
Phone No. :		
Address :		

Document Type :	Date Notarized :	Document Date :	Fee Charged :

ID Number :	Identification :	Service Performed :
	☐ ID Card ☐ Witness	☐ Jurat ☐ Oath
	☐ Known Personally	☐ Acknowledgement
Issued By :	☐ Driver's License ☐ Passport	
Date Issued : Expiration Date :	☐ Others	☐ Others

Witness Name :	Address :
Email Address :	Phone No. :
Witness Signature :	NOTE :

❖ NOTARY LOGBOOK ❖ / 170

Printed Name :	Signer's Signature :	Thumb Print :
Email Address :		
Phone No. :		
Address :		

Document Type :	Date Notarized :	Document Date :	Fee Charged :

ID Number :	Identification :	Service Performed :
	☐ ID Card ☐ Witness	☐ Jurat ☐ Oath
	☐ Known Personally	☐ Acknowledgement
Issued By :	☐ Driver's License ☐ Passport	
Date Issued : Expiration Date :	☐ Others	☐ Others

Witness Name :	Address :
Email Address :	Phone No. :
Witness Signature :	NOTE :

Printed Name :

Email Address :

Phone No. :

Address :

Signer's Signature :

Thumb Print :

Document Type :	Date Notarized :	Document Date :	Fee Charged :

ID Number :

Issued By :

Date Issued :

Expiration Date :

Identification :
- ☐ ID Card
- ☐ Known Personally
- ☐ Driver's License
- ☐ Witness
- ☐ Passport
- ☐ Others

Service Performed :
- ☐ Jurat
- ☐ Oath
- ☐ Acknowledgement
- ☐ Others

Witness Name :

Address :

Email Address :

Phone No. :

Witness Signature :

NOTE :

Printed Name :

Email Address :

Phone No. :

Address :

Signer's Signature :

Thumb Print :

Document Type :	Date Notarized :	Document Date :	Fee Charged :

ID Number :

Issued By :

Date Issued :

Expiration Date :

Identification :
- ☐ ID Card
- ☐ Known Personally
- ☐ Driver's License
- ☐ Witness
- ☐ Passport
- ☐ Others

Service Performed :
- ☐ Jurat
- ☐ Oath
- ☐ Acknowledgement
- ☐ Others

Witness Name :

Address :

Email Address :

Phone No. :

Witness Signature :

NOTE :

⇢ NOTARY LOGBOOK ⇠ 173

Printed Name :

Email Address :

Phone No. :

Address :

Signer's Signature :

Thumb Print :

Document Type :	Date Notarized :	Document Date :	Fee Charged :

ID Number :

Issued By :

Date Issued :　Expiration Date :

Identification :
- ☐ ID Card　☐ Witness
- ☐ Known Personally
- ☐ Driver's License　☐ Passport
- ☐ Others

Service Performed :
- ☐ Jurat　☐ Oath
- ☐ Acknowledgement
- ☐ Others

Witness Name :

Address :

Email Address :

Phone No. :

Witness Signature :

NOTE :

⇢ NOTARY LOGBOOK ⇠ 174

Printed Name :

Email Address :

Phone No. :

Address :

Signer's Signature :

Thumb Print :

Document Type :	Date Notarized :	Document Date :	Fee Charged :

ID Number :

Issued By :

Date Issued :　Expiration Date :

Identification :
- ☐ ID Card　☐ Witness
- ☐ Known Personally
- ☐ Driver's License　☐ Passport
- ☐ Others

Service Performed :
- ☐ Jurat　☐ Oath
- ☐ Acknowledgement
- ☐ Others

Witness Name :

Address :

Email Address :

Phone No. :

Witness Signature :

NOTE :

Printed Name :

Email Address :

Phone No. :

Address :

Signer's Signature :

Thumb Print :

Document Type :	Date Notarized :	Document Date :	Fee Charged :

ID Number :

Issued By :

Date Issued :	Expiration Date :

Identification :
- ☐ ID Card
- ☐ Witness
- ☐ Known Personally
- ☐ Driver's License
- ☐ Passport
- ☐ Others

Service Performed :
- ☐ Jurat
- ☐ Oath
- ☐ Acknowledgement
- ☐ Others

Witness Name :

Email Address :

Witness Signature :

Address :

Phone No. :

NOTE :

Printed Name :

Email Address :

Phone No. :

Address :

Signer's Signature :

Thumb Print :

Document Type :	Date Notarized :	Document Date :	Fee Charged :

ID Number :

Issued By :

Date Issued :	Expiration Date :

Identification :
- ☐ ID Card
- ☐ Witness
- ☐ Known Personally
- ☐ Driver's License
- ☐ Passport
- ☐ Others

Service Performed :
- ☐ Jurat
- ☐ Oath
- ☐ Acknowledgement
- ☐ Others

Witness Name :

Email Address :

Witness Signature :

Address :

Phone No. :

NOTE :

Printed Name :

Email Address :

Phone No. :

Address :

Signer's Signature :

Thumb Print :

Document Type :	Date Notarized :	Document Date :	Fee Charged :

ID Number :

Issued By :

Date Issued :	Expiration Date :

Identification :
- ☐ ID Card
- ☐ Known Personally
- ☐ Driver's License
- ☐ Witness
- ☐ Passport
- ☐ Others

Service Performed :
- ☐ Jurat
- ☐ Oath
- ☐ Acknowledgement
- ☐ Others

Witness Name :

Address :

Email Address :

Phone No. :

Witness Signature :

NOTE :

Printed Name :

Email Address :

Phone No. :

Address :

Signer's Signature :

Thumb Print :

Document Type :	Date Notarized :	Document Date :	Fee Charged :

ID Number :

Issued By :

Date Issued :	Expiration Date :

Identification :
- ☐ ID Card
- ☐ Known Personally
- ☐ Driver's License
- ☐ Witness
- ☐ Passport
- ☐ Others

Service Performed :
- ☐ Jurat
- ☐ Oath
- ☐ Acknowledgement
- ☐ Others

Witness Name :

Address :

Email Address :

Phone No. :

Witness Signature :

NOTE :

❖ NOTARY LOGBOOK ❖ / 179

Printed Name :

Email Address :

Phone No. :

Address :

Signer's Signature :

Thumb Print :

Document Type :	Date Notarized :	Document Date :	Fee Charged :

ID Number :

Issued By :

Date Issued : | Expiration Date :

Identification :
- ☐ ID Card   ☐ Witness
- ☐ Known Personally
- ☐ Driver's License   ☐ Passport
- ☐ Others

Service Performed :
- ☐ Jurat   ☐ Oath
- ☐ Acknowledgement
- ☐ Others

Witness Name :

Address :

Email Address :

Phone No. :

Witness Signature :

NOTE :

❖ NOTARY LOGBOOK ❖ / 180

Printed Name :

Email Address :

Phone No. :

Address :

Signer's Signature :

Thumb Print :

Document Type :	Date Notarized :	Document Date :	Fee Charged :

ID Number :

Issued By :

Date Issued : | Expiration Date :

Identification :
- ☐ ID Card   ☐ Witness
- ☐ Known Personally
- ☐ Driver's License   ☐ Passport
- ☐ Others

Service Performed :
- ☐ Jurat   ☐ Oath
- ☐ Acknowledgement
- ☐ Others

Witness Name :

Address :

Email Address :

Phone No. :

Witness Signature :

NOTE :

← NOTARY LOGBOOK ← 181

Printed Name :

Email Address :

Phone No. :

Address :

Signer's Signature :

Thumb Print :

Document Type :	Date Notarized :	Document Date :	Fee Charged :

ID Number :

Issued By :

Date Issued :	Expiration Date :

Identification :
- ☐ ID Card
- ☐ Witness
- ☐ Known Personally
- ☐ Driver's License
- ☐ Passport
- ☐ Others

Service Performed :
- ☐ Jurat
- ☐ Oath
- ☐ Acknowledgement
- ☐ Others

Witness Name :

Email Address :

Witness Signature :

Address :

Phone No. :

NOTE :

← NOTARY LOGBOOK ← 182

Printed Name :

Email Address :

Phone No. :

Address :

Signer's Signature :

Thumb Print :

Document Type :	Date Notarized :	Document Date :	Fee Charged :

ID Number :

Issued By :

Date Issued :	Expiration Date :

Identification :
- ☐ ID Card
- ☐ Witness
- ☐ Known Personally
- ☐ Driver's License
- ☐ Passport
- ☐ Others

Service Performed :
- ☐ Jurat
- ☐ Oath
- ☐ Acknowledgement
- ☐ Others

Witness Name :

Email Address :

Witness Signature :

Address :

Phone No. :

NOTE :

→ NOTARY LOGBOOK ← 183

Printed Name :

Email Address :

Phone No. :

Address :

Signer's Signature :

Thumb Print :

Document Type :	Date Notarized :	Document Date :	Fee Charged :

ID Number :

Issued By :

Date Issued :

Expiration Date :

Identification :
- ☐ ID Card
- ☐ Witness
- ☐ Known Personally
- ☐ Driver's License
- ☐ Passport
- ☐ Others

Service Performed :
- ☐ Jurat
- ☐ Oath
- ☐ Acknowledgement
- ☐ Others

Witness Name :

Email Address :

Witness Signature :

Address :

Phone No. :

NOTE :

→ NOTARY LOGBOOK ← 184

Printed Name :

Email Address :

Phone No. :

Address :

Signer's Signature :

Thumb Print :

Document Type :	Date Notarized :	Document Date :	Fee Charged :

ID Number :

Issued By :

Date Issued :

Expiration Date :

Identification :
- ☐ ID Card
- ☐ Witness
- ☐ Known Personally
- ☐ Driver's License
- ☐ Passport
- ☐ Others

Service Performed :
- ☐ Jurat
- ☐ Oath
- ☐ Acknowledgement
- ☐ Others

Witness Name :

Email Address :

Witness Signature :

Address :

Phone No. :

NOTE :

Printed Name :

Email Address :

Phone No. :

Address :

Signer's Signature :

Thumb Print :

Document Type :	Date Notarized :	Document Date :	Fee Charged :

ID Number :

Issued By :

Date Issued :	Expiration Date :

Identification :
- ☐ ID Card   ☐ Witness
- ☐ Known Personally
- ☐ Driver's License   ☐ Passport
- ☐ Others

Service Performed :
- ☐ Jurat   ☐ Oath
- ☐ Acknowledgement
- ☐ Others

Witness Name :

Email Adress :

Witness Signature :

Address :

Phone No. :

NOTE :

Printed Name :

Email Address :

Phone No. :

Address :

Signer's Signature :

Thumb Print :

Document Type :	Date Notarized :	Document Date :	Fee Charged :

ID Number :

Issued By :

Date Issued :	Expiration Date :

Identification :
- ☐ ID Card   ☐ Witness
- ☐ Known Personally
- ☐ Driver's License   ☐ Passport
- ☐ Others

Service Performed :
- ☐ Jurat   ☐ Oath
- ☐ Acknowledgement
- ☐ Others

Witness Name :

Email Address :

Witness Signature :

Address :

Phone No. :

NOTE :

☙ NOTARY LOGBOOK ❧ / 187

Printed Name :

Email Address :

Phone No. :

Address :

Signer's Signature :

Thumb Print :

Document Type : Date Notarized : Document Date : Fee Charged :

ID Number :

Issued By :

Date Issued : Expiration Date :

Identification :
- ☐ ID Card   ☐ Witness
- ☐ Known Personally
- ☐ Driver's License   ☐ Passport
- ☐ Others

Service Performed :
- ☐ Jurat   ☐ Oath
- ☐ Acknowledgement
- ☐ Others

Witness Name :

Email Address :

Witness Signature :

Address :

Phone No. :

NOTE :

☙ NOTARY LOGBOOK ❧ / 188

Printed Name :

Email Address :

Phone No. :

Address :

Signer's Signature :

Thumb Print :

Document Type : Date Notarized : Document Date : Fee Charged :

ID Number :

Issued By :

Date Issued : Expiration Date :

Identification :
- ☐ ID Card   ☐ Witness
- ☐ Known Personally
- ☐ Driver's License   ☐ Passport
- ☐ Others

Service Performed :
- ☐ Jurat   ☐ Oath
- ☐ Acknowledgement
- ☐ Others

Witness Name :

Email Address :

Witness Signature :

Address :

Phone No. :

NOTE :

➤ NOTARY LOGBOOK ➤ / 189

Printed Name :

Email Address :

Phone No. :

Address :

Signer's Signature :

Thumb Print :

Document Type :	Date Notarized :	Document Date :	Fee Charged :

ID Number :

Issued By :

Date Issued :	Expiration Date :

Identification :
- ☐ ID Card
- ☐ Witness
- ☐ Known Personally
- ☐ Driver's License
- ☐ Passport
- ☐ Others

Service Performed :
- ☐ Jurat
- ☐ Oath
- ☐ Acknowledgement
- ☐ Others

Witness Name :

Address :

Email Address :

Phone No. :

Witness Signature :

NOTE :

➤ NOTARY LOGBOOK ➤ / 190

Printed Name :

Email Address :

Phone No. :

Address :

Signer's Signature :

Thumb Print :

Document Type :	Date Notarized :	Document Date :	Fee Charged :

ID Number :

Issued By :

Date Issued :	Expiration Date :

Identification :
- ☐ ID Card
- ☐ Witness
- ☐ Known Personally
- ☐ Driver's License
- ☐ Passport
- ☐ Others

Service Performed :
- ☐ Jurat
- ☐ Oath
- ☐ Acknowledgement
- ☐ Others

Witness Name :

Address :

Email Address :

Phone No. :

Witness Signature :

NOTE :

❖ NOTARY LOGBOOK ❖ / 191

Printed Name :

Email Address :

Phone No. :

Address :

Signer's Signature :

Thumb Print :

Document Type :	Date Notarized :	Document Date :	Fee Charged :

ID Number :

Issued By :

Date Issued : | Expiration Date :

Identification :
- ☐ ID Card ☐ Witness
- ☐ Known Personally
- ☐ Driver's License ☐ Passport
- ☐ Others

Service Performed :
- ☐ Jurat ☐ Oath
- ☐ Acknowledgement
- ☐ Others

Witness Name :

Email Address :

Witness Signature :

Address :

Phone No. :

NOTE :

❖ NOTARY LOGBOOK ❖ / 192

Printed Name :

Email Address :

Phone No. :

Address :

Signer's Signature :

Thumb Print :

Document Type :	Date Notarized :	Document Date :	Fee Charged :

ID Number :

Issued By :

Date Issued : | Expiration Date :

Identification :
- ☐ ID Card ☐ Witness
- ☐ Known Personally
- ☐ Driver's License ☐ Passport
- ☐ Others

Service Performed :
- ☐ Jurat ☐ Oath
- ☐ Acknowledgement
- ☐ Others

Witness Name :

Email Address :

Witness Signature :

Address :

Phone No. :

NOTE :

✦ NOTARY LOGBOOK ✦

Printed Name :

Email Address :

Phone No. :

Address :

Signer's Signature :

Thumb Print :

Document Type :	Date Notarized :	Document Date :	Fee Charged :

ID Number :

Issued By :

Date Issued :   Expiration Date :

Identification :
- ☐ ID Card   ☐ Witness
- ☐ Known Personally
- ☐ Driver's License ☐ Passport
- ☐ Others

Service Performed :
- ☐ Jurat   ☐ Oath
- ☐ Acknowledgement
- ☐ Others

Witness Name :

Email Address :

Witness Signature :

Address :

Phone No. :

NOTE :

✦ NOTARY LOGBOOK ✦

Printed Name :

Email Address :

Phone No. :

Address :

Signer's Signature :

Thumb Print :

Document Type :	Date Notarized :	Document Date :	Fee Charged :

ID Number :

Issued By :

Date Issued :   Expiration Date :

Identification :
- ☐ ID Card   ☐ Witness
- ☐ Known Personally
- ☐ Driver's License ☐ Passport
- ☐ Others

Service Performed :
- ☐ Jurat   ☐ Oath
- ☐ Acknowledgement
- ☐ Others

Witness Name :

Email Address :

Witness Signature :

Address :

Phone No. :

NOTE :

Printed Name :

Signer's Signature :

Thumb Print :

Email Address :

Phone No. :

Address :

Document Type :	Date Notarized :	Document Date :	Fee Charged :

ID Number :	Identification :	Service Performed :

Issued By :

☐ ID Card   ☐ Witness
☐ Known Personally
☐ Driver's License   ☐ Passport
☐ Others

☐ Jurat   ☐ Oath
☐ Acknowledgement

☐ Others

Date Issued :	Expiration Date :

Witness Name :

Address :

Email Address :

Phone No. :

Witness Signature :

NOTE :

Printed Name :

Signer's Signature :

Thumb Print :

Email Address :

Phone No. :

Address :

Document Type :	Date Notarized :	Document Date :	Fee Charged :

ID Number :	Identification :	Service Performed :

Issued By :

☐ ID Card   ☐ Witness
☐ Known Personally
☐ Driver's License   ☐ Passport
☐ Others

☐ Jurat   ☐ Oath
☐ Acknowledgement

☐ Others

Date Issued :	Expiration Date :

Witness Name :

Address :

Email Address :

Phone No. :

Witness Signature :

NOTE :

✦ NOTARY LOGBOOK ✦ / 197

Printed Name :

Email Address :

Phone No. :

Address :

Signer's Signature :

Thumb Print :

Document Type :	Date Notarized :	Document Date :	Fee Charged :

ID Number :

Issued By :

Date Issued :	Expiration Date :

Identification :
- ☐ ID Card
- ☐ Known Personally
- ☐ Driver's License
- ☐ Witness
- ☐ Passport
- ☐ Others

Service Performed :
- ☐ Jurat
- ☐ Oath
- ☐ Acknowledgement
- ☐ Others

Witness Name :

Email Address :

Witness Signature :

Address :

Phone No. :

NOTE :

✦ NOTARY LOGBOOK ✦ / 198

Printed Name :

Email Address :

Phone No. :

Address :

Signer's Signature :

Thumb Print :

Document Type :	Date Notarized :	Document Date :	Fee Charged :

ID Number :

Issued By :

Date Issued :	Expiration Date :

Identification :
- ☐ ID Card
- ☐ Known Personally
- ☐ Driver's License
- ☐ Witness
- ☐ Passport
- ☐ Others

Service Performed :
- ☐ Jurat
- ☐ Oath
- ☐ Acknowledgement
- ☐ Others

Witness Name :

Email Address :

Witness Signature :

Address :

Phone No. :

NOTE :

→ NOTARY LOGBOOK ← / 199

Printed Name :

Email Address :

Phone No. :

Address :

Signer's Signature :

Thumb Print :

Document Type :	Date Notarized :	Document Date :	Fee Charged :

ID Number :

Issued By :

Date Issued :	Expiration Date :

Identification :
- ☐ ID Card   ☐ Witness
- ☐ Known Personally
- ☐ Driver's License ☐ Passport
- ☐ Others

Service Performed :
- ☐ Jurat   ☐ Oath
- ☐ Acknowledgement
- ☐ Others

Witness Name :

Email Address :

Witness Signature :

Address :

Phone No. :

NOTE :

→ NOTARY LOGBOOK ← / 200

Printed Name :

Email Address :

Phone No. :

Address :

Signer's Signature :

Thumb Print :

Document Type :	Date Notarized :	Document Date :	Fee Charged :

ID Number :

Issued By :

Date Issued :	Expiration Date :

Identification :
- ☐ ID Card   ☐ Witness
- ☐ Known Personally
- ☐ Driver's License ☐ Passport
- ☐ Others

Service Performed :
- ☐ Jurat   ☐ Oath
- ☐ Acknowledgement
- ☐ Others

Witness Name :

Email Address :

Witness Signature :

Address :

Phone No. :

NOTE :

Made in the USA
Las Vegas, NV
06 November 2024